Microsoft®
Outlook®
2002

M I N U T E

G U I D E

201 West 103rd Street
Indianapolis, IN 46290

Joe Habraken

10 Minute Guide to Microsoft® Outlook® 2002

Copyright © 2002 by Que® Corporation

International Standard Book Number: 0-7897-2638-6

Library of Congress Catalog Card Number: 20-01090289

Printed in the United States of America

First Printing: August 2001

04   03   02   7

Trademarks

All terms mentioned in this book that are known to be trademarks or service marks have been appropriately capitalized. Que cannot attest to the accuracy of this information. Use of a term in this book should not be regarded as affecting the validity of any trademark or service mark.

Warning and Disclaimer

Associate Publisher
Greg Wiegand

Managing Editor
Thomas Hayes

Acquisitions Editor
Stephanie J. McComb

Development Editor
Stephanie J. McComb

Project Editor
Tricia Liebig

Indexer
Mandie Frank

Proofreaders
Angela Boley
Amy Jay

Team Coordinator
Sharry Lee Gregory

Interior Designer
Gary Adair

Cover Designer
Alan Clements

Page Layout
Lizbeth Patterson

Contents

DEDICATION

To my Aunt Donna; enjoy your retirement!

ACKNOWLEDGMENTS

Creating books like this takes a real team effort. I would like to thank Stephanie McComb, our acquisitions editor, who worked very hard to assemble the team that made this book a reality and also served as the development editor for this book—coming up with many great ideas for improving the content of the book. Also, a great big thanks to our project editor, Tricia Liebig, who ran the last leg of the race and made sure the book made it to press on time—what a great team of professionals.

TELL US WHAT YOU THINK!

As the reader of this book, *you* are our most important critic and commentator. We value your opinion and want to know what we're doing right, what we could do better, what areas you'd like to see us publish in, and any other words of wisdom you're willing to pass our way.

As an Associate Publisher for Que, I welcome your comments. You can fax, e-mail, or write me directly to let me know what you did or didn't like about this book—as well as what we can do to make our books stronger.

Please note that I cannot help you with technical problems related to the topic of this book, and that due to the high volume of mail I receive, I might not be able to reply to every message.

When you write, please be sure to include this book's title and author as well as your name and phone or fax number. I will carefully review your comments and share them with the author and editors who worked on the book.

Fax: 317-581-4666

E-mail: feedback@quepublishing.com

Mail: Greg Wiegand
            Que
            201 West 103rd Street
            Indianapolis, IN 46290 USA

Introduction

Microsoft Outlook 2002 is a personal information manager (PIM). With Outlook, you can communicate throughout your office or over the Internet with e-mail, and you can also schedule meetings, create task lists for yourself and others and keep track of all your important appointments. Outlook provides accessibility and flexibility for you and your coworkers and friends.

THE WHAT AND WHY OF MICROSOFT OUTLOOK

Outlook can help you organize your work on a day-to-day basis. Using Microsoft Outlook, you can do the following:

- Create task lists

- Manage your calendar

- Log phone calls and other important events in your journal

- Make notes to remind yourself of important tasks

Additionally, Outlook can help you communicate with others and share your workload. When you and your coworkers use the combined features of Microsoft Outlook and Microsoft Office, you can

- Schedule meetings and invite coworkers

- Communicate with others using e-mail

- Import and export files

While providing you with many communication and organizational features, Microsoft Outlook is easy to learn. This book will help you understand the possibilities awaiting you with Microsoft Outlook 2002.

WHY QUE'S *10 MINUTE GUIDE TO MICROSOFT OUTLOOK 2002?*

The 10 Minute Guide to Microsoft Outlook 2002 can save you precious time while you get to know the different features provided by Microsoft Outlook. Each lesson is designed to be completed in 10 minutes or less, so you'll be up to snuff on basic and advanced Outlook features quickly.

Although you can jump around among lessons, starting at the beginning is a good plan. The bare-bones basics are covered first, and more advanced topics are covered later. If you need help installing Outlook, see the next section for instructions.

WHO SHOULD USE THIS BOOK?

The *10 Minute Guide to Microsoft Outlook 2002* is for anyone who

*   Has Microsoft Outlook 2002 installed on their PC.

*   Needs to learn Microsoft Outlook 2002 quickly.

*   Wants to explore some of the advanced features of Outlook.

*   Wants a quick way to select, learn, and perform tasks in Microsoft Outlook.

CONVENTIONS USED IN THIS BOOK

The *10 Minute Guide to Microsoft Outlook 2002* includes step-by-step instructions for performing specific tasks. To help you as you work through these steps and help you move through the lessons easily, additional information is included and identified by the following icons.

> **PLAIN ENGLISH**
> New or unfamiliar terms are defined to help you as you work through the various steps in the lesson.

TIP

Read these tips for ideas that cut corners and confusion.

CAUTION

This icon identifies areas where new users often run into trouble; these hints offer practical solutions to those problems.

LESSON 1
What's New in Outlook 2002?

In this lesson, you are introduced to Outlook's powerful organizing features, and you learn what's new in Outlook 2002.

GETTING ORGANIZED WITH OUTLOOK 2002

Outlook 2002 is the latest version of Microsoft's popular personal information manager (PIM). Outlook can help you manage incoming and outgoing e-mail messages and help you keep organized by providing a personal calendar, a contacts list, and a personal to-do list. Since Outlook's ultimate purpose is to keep you organized, its basic "look and feel" makes it easy for you to manage your e-mail, contacts, and appointments.

PLAIN ENGLISH

Personal Information Manager (PIM) A PIM is a software package that helps you keep track of your appointments, meetings, contacts, and messages, such as e-mail and faxes.

Outlook provides an environment that's very much like a filing cabinet. Items of information are kept in folders, which you can access with one click of the mouse. For instance, your new e-mail messages can be found in the Inbox. Appointments, meetings, and events are stored in the Calendar folder. The names of your contacts, their e-mail addresses, business addresses, and phone numbers are stored in the

Contacts folder. Folders are also provided for your Tasks, Journal Entries, and Notes.

NEW FEATURES IN OUTLOOK 2002

On the surface Outlook 2002 looks very similar to the previous version of Outlook, Outlook 2000. For example, Outlook 2002 uses the same adaptive menu and toolbar system found in Outlook 2000 that customizes the commands listed on the menu system and icons available on toolbars based on the commands you use most frequently.

You will find, however, that Outlook 2002 offers a number of improvements over previous versions of Outlook. These improvements range from an easier setup procedure for your e-mail accounts to the availability of AutoCorrect to automatically detect and correct spelling errors and typos in your messages and other entries. Let's take a look at some of the new enhancements available in Outlook 2002.

EASIER E-MAIL CONFIGURATION

In Outlook 2000, the Outlook Startup Wizard required that you selected the type of network environment that Outlook would be used in: either a corporate network that used a Microsoft Exchange Server to handle e-mail or a stand-alone computer connected to the Internet. Outlook 2002 no longer requires that you make the distinction between Outlook on a corporate network or as an Internet e-mail client.

Outlook 2002 also makes it much easier for you to add different kinds of e-mail accounts and access them from the Outlook Inbox. Not only are Exchange Server e-mail accounts and Internet e-mail accounts supported, but you can now use Outlook as your e-mail client for World Wide Web e-mail services such as Microsoft Hotmail. Once you have Outlook 2002 up and running, your e-mail accounts can be added, edited, or removed using the new E-mail Accounts Wizard. Adding and configuring e-mail accounts is covered in Lesson 3, "Understanding the Outlook E-mail Configurations."

FRIENDLY NAMES DISPLAYED IN E-MAILS

When you add contacts to your Contacts folder, you can now enter a "friendly name" for the contact. This friendly name, which is entered in the Display As box in the Contact's window (see Figure 1.1), will then appear in the To: box when you send an e-mail to the contact.

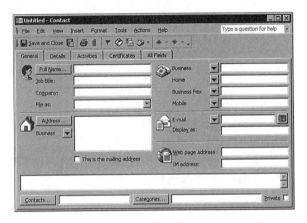

FIGURE 1.1
Friendly names can be specified for your contacts.

Using friendly names to identify contacts allows you to make sure that you are sending a particular e-mail message to the correct contact. Creating a Contacts list is covered in Lesson 13, "Creating a Contacts List."

OTHER OUTLOOK 2002 ENHANCEMENTS

Outlook 2002 also provides other enhancements that make it easier to use than previous versions of Outlook. Some of these enhancements are:

- **Microsoft Word Is the Default E-mail Editor**   If you have Microsoft Word 2002 installed on your computer, Outlook is configured to use Word as its default e-mail editor. This allows you to take advantage of Word's powerful word-processing features to create your e-mails. E-mails are created by default as HTML documents, which allow you to format text in the message and even include images directly in the e-mail message.

- **AutoCorrect Available**   AutoCorrect automatically detects and correct typos, misspellings, and incorrect capitalization. Even if you decide not to use Word as your e-mail editor, Outlook still allows you to take advantage of the AutoCorrect feature as you compose your e-mail messages.

- **Extra Line Breaks Removed from Text Messages**   Many text messages that you receive as e-mail will contain extra line breaks that make the message difficult to read. Outlook 2002 automatically removes these extra line breaks; this makes it easier for you to read the text-only messages that you receive in your Inbox.

- **Preview Pane Can Be Used to Open Attachments and Follow Links**   The Preview pane in Outlook 2002 now allows you to click on links contained in e-mail messages and follow these links to Web addresses. Attachments contained in an e-mail message can also be opened directly from the Preview pane.

CAUTION

Outlook 2002 No Longer Emphasized As Fax Manager   An additional change that you will find in Outlook 2002 is that it does not include a new version of WinFax. While previous versions of WinFax included as part of earlier versions of Outlook are supported, Outlook 2002 is probably no longer your best tool for sending, receiving, and managing fax messages. A third party fax service will provide you greater flexibility when working with faxes.

Outlook 2002 provides more features and greater ease of use than previous versions of this powerful PIM. This book will provide you with step-by-step lessons that you can use to familiarize yourself with the various organizational features provided by Outlook.

In this lesson, you learned how Outlook can help you stay organized. You were also introduced to some of the new features found in Outlook 2002. In the next lesson, you will take a first look at the Outlook window and learn how to start and exit the software.

LESSON 2

Getting Started
in Outlook

In this lesson, you learn how to start and exit Outlook, identify parts
of the Outlook window, and use the mouse to get around the program.

STARTING OUTLOOK

You start Outlook from the Windows desktop. After starting the program, you can leave it open, or you can minimize it to free up the desktop for other applications. Either way, you can access it at any time during your day.

CAUTION

> **Outlook and System Performance**   If you leave Outlook open on your desktop, it still requires a certain amount of your system resources. This means that if you normally run multiple applications, such as Word and Excel, you might see some loss of performance as you work. If this becomes a problem, close Outlook (or any program not being used) to free up your system's memory. Adding memory to your system, of course, also is an alternative for increasing performance. The suggested amount of memory for running Office XP is 64MB for Windows 98, Me, and Windows NT. For Windows 2000, 128MB is suggested.

To start Microsoft Outlook, follow these steps:

1. From the Windows desktop, click the **Start** button, choose **Programs**, and then select **Microsoft Outlook**.

Shortcuts to Launching Outlook   You can also double-click the **Outlook** shortcut icon on the desktop to start Outlook, or you can click the **Outlook** icon on the Quick Launch toolbar on the Windows taskbar (next to the Start button).

2. If your PC is set up for multiple users, the Choose Profile dialog box appears; click **OK** to accept the default profile, or choose your profile and open Microsoft Outlook. Figure 2.1 shows the Outlook screen that appears.

Profile   The profile includes information about you and your e-mail accounts and is created automatically when you install Outlook (the e-mail accounts are added to the profile when Outlook is set up for the first time, as discussed in Lesson 3, "Understanding the Outlook E-mail Configurations"). Multiple profiles become an issue only if you share your computer with other users.

In situations where you connect to the Internet using a modem dial-up connection, the Connection Wizard attempts to make a dial-in connection as Outlook opens. This enables Outlook to check your e-mail server.

The First Time You Start Outlook   The very first time you start Outlook on a computer that has not had a previous version of the software installed, you will be required to configure the e-mail accounts that you use. Setting up your e-mail accounts is discussed in Lesson 3.

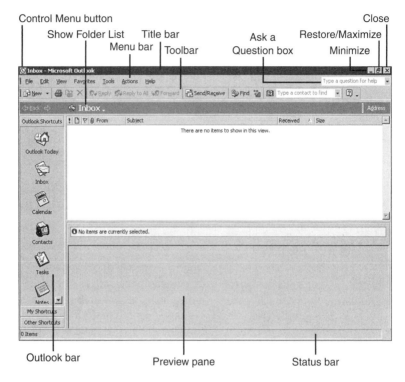

Control Menu button

Show Folder List   Title bar

Menu bar   Toolbar

Ask a
Question box

Close

Restore/Maximize

Minimize

Outlook bar   Preview pane   Status bar

FIGURE 2.1
The Outlook window includes all the icons and items you need to access its various features.

UNDERSTANDING THE OUTLOOK WINDOW

The Outlook window includes items you can use to navigate in and operate the program. If you do not see some of the items listed in Figure 2.1 on your screen, open the **View** menu and select the command for the appropriate element (such as **Toolbars**, **Status Bar**, **Folder List**, or **Outlook Bar**). A check mark in front of an item means the item is currently showing. If you find the Preview pane distracting when you first open the Outlook window, click the **View** menu and click **Preview Pane** to close the Preview pane.

Table 2.1 describes the elements you see in the opening screen.

TABLE 2.1   Elements of the Outlook Window

Element	Description
Title bar	Includes the name of the application and current folder, plus the Minimize, Maximize, and Close buttons.
Control Menu button	Opens the Control menu, which provides such commands as Move, Size, Minimize, and Close.
Minimize button	Reduces the Outlook window to a button on the taskbar; to restore the window to its original size, click the button on the taskbar.
Maximize button	Enlarges the Outlook window to cover the Windows desktop. When the window is maximized, the Maximize button changes to a Restore button you can click to return the window to its previous size.
Close (x) button	Closes the Outlook program window.
Menu bar	Contains menus of commands you can use to perform tasks in the program.
Toolbar	Includes icons that serve as shortcuts for common commands, such as creating a new message or printing a message.
Show Folder List	Displays the current folder. Click this to display a list of personal folders you can open.
Outlook bar	Displays icons representing folders: Inbox, Calendar, Contacts, and so on. Click an icon to change to the folder it names. The Outlook Shortcuts, My Shortcuts, and Other Shortcuts buttons on the bar list specific groups of folders (for example, the My Shortcuts button lists icons related to your e-mail, such as the Drafts, Outbox, and Sent items).

TABLE 2.1   (continued)

Element	Description
Status bar	Displays information about the items currently shown in the Information Viewer.
Preview pane	Displays a preview of the currently selected item in your Outlook Inbox or other selected folder.
Ask a Question box	This box allows you to quickly ask the Outlook Help system a question. It also allows you to forgo using the Office Assistant to access the Help system.

TIP

Finding a Toolbar Button's Purpose   You can place the mouse pointer on any toolbar button to view a description of that tool's function.

Using the Mouse in Outlook

Like most Windows-based programs, you can use the mouse in Outlook to select items, open e-mail and folders, move items, and so on. In general, clicking selects an item, and double-clicking selects it and performs some action on it (for example, displaying its contents). In addition to clicking and double-clicking, there are some special mouse actions you can use in Outlook:

- **Drag**—To move an object to another position on the screen (to transfer a mail message to another folder, for example), you can drag the object with the mouse. To drag an object to a new location onscreen, point to the object and press and hold down the left mouse button. Move the mouse pointer to the new location and then release the mouse button.

- **Right-click**—You can display a shortcut menu by clicking the right mouse button when pointing to an item. For example, you can right-click a folder in the Outlook bar or a piece of e-mail. A shortcut menu appears, which usually contains common commands relating to that particular item.

- **Multiselect**—You can act on multiple items at once by selecting them before issuing a command. To select multiple contiguous items, hold down the **Shift** key and click the first and last items you want to select. To select noncontiguous items (those that are not adjacent to each other), hold down the **Ctrl** key and click each item.

If you have a mouse, such as the Microsoft IntelliMouse, that includes a scroll wheel, you can use it in Outlook. Turn the wheel toward you to move down through any list in Outlook, such as your Contacts list, or move the wheel up to scroll up in a list.

TIP

Keyboard Shortcuts   You can use the keyboard to move around Outlook and to access many, but not all, of its features. For example, to open a menu with the keyboard, press the **Alt** key and then press the underlined letter in the menu name (press **Alt+F** to open the File menu, for instance).

WORKING OFFLINE

In cases where you use a modem connection to access your e-mail server, you can close the connection while still working in Outlook. This allows you to free up your phone line or, if you pay for your connection based on the time you are connected, save on connection time. Working offline in Outlook does not affect any Outlook features or capabilities. E-mail that you create while working offline is held in the Outbox until you reconnect to your Internet connection.

To work offline, select the **File** menu and then select **Work Offline**. If you are prompted to confirm the closing of your dial-in connection, click **Yes**.

EXITING OUTLOOK

When you are finished working in Outlook, you can exit the application in a couple of ways. You can use the File menu: select **File, Exit**. Or you can close Outlook by clicking the Outlook window's **Close (x)** button. In cases where you are connected to the Internet using a dial-up connection, you are prompted as to whether you want to log off your connection. If you want to close the dial-up connection, select **Log Off** in the message box.

In this lesson, you learned about the Outlook window, how to start and exit Outlook, and how to use the mouse to get around the program. In the next lesson, you will learn about the different Outlook e-mail account types and how to add them to the Outlook configuration. You also will learn how to access e-mail accounts to edit their settings and how to delete unneeded e-mail accounts.

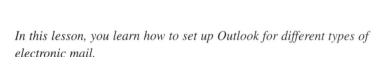

LESSON 3

Understanding the Outlook E-mail Configurations

In this lesson, you learn how to set up Outlook for different types of electronic mail.

TYPES OF OUTLOOK E-MAIL CONFIGURATIONS

The type or flavor of e-mail that you use in Outlook depends on who provides your e-mail account. Outlook contains support for the three most common providers of e-mail service:

- **ISP**—When you sign up for an Internet service provider (ISP), the company usually provides you with at least one e-mail account.

- **Exchange**—In networked environments (most offices, for example), an e-mail server such as Microsoft Exchange may control delivery of e-mail.

- **Web**—Outlook also provides you with the capability to connect to Web-based e-mail services, such as Microsoft's Hotmail or Yahoo!'s Yahoo! mail.

Because Outlook serves not only as your e-mail client, but also as your personal information manager (allowing you to build a contacts list and keep track of your appointments and tasks), it is designed to operate either in a standalone environment or in a corporate service environment. As a standalone application, your contacts, appointments, and tasks are stored locally on your computer and you access your e-mail through the Internet. However, in a corporate environment, your calendar and tasks folders are kept on a corporate communication server (typically Microsoft Exchange Server) where your information can be shared with other users.

PLAIN ENGLISH

> **E-mail Client**   Software that is configured on a user's computer to connect to e-mail services on a company's network or on the Internet.

MAKING YOUR E-MAIL CHOICE

The first time you start Outlook (double-click its desktop icon), you must communicate to Outlook the type of e-mail account that you use on your computer. Outlook assists you in this task by launching the Outlook Startup Wizard. Click **Next** to move past the opening screen. The E-mail Accounts screen appears as shown in Figure 3.1.

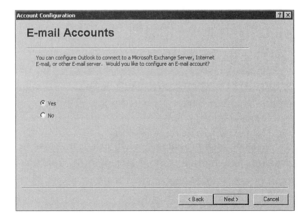

FIGURE 3.1
The Outlook Startup Wizard helps you set up your e-mail accounts.

To configure an e-mail account for use in Outlook, make sure that the **Yes** option button is selected, and then click **Next** to continue. The next screen presents a selection of different e-mail servers, as shown in Figure 3.2.

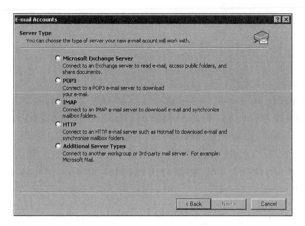

FIGURE 3.2
Outlook can function as an e-mail client for several e-mail types.

How your e-mail functions depends on which option you select to configure Outlook as a specific e-mail client. The possibilities are

- **Microsoft Exchange Server**—This type of account makes Outlook an Exchange Server client; mailboxes and other resources, such as shared public folders, are managed on the Exchange Server computer. If this is what your Outlook installation requires, your network system administrator should provide these settings for you.

- **POP3**—POP3 is a protocol that most ISPs use, which allows a POP3 e-mail server to function as a mail drop.

  This means that your Internet e-mail is forwarded to the POP3 server and sits there until you connect with your e-mail client (Outlook) and download the mail to your computer.

PLAIN ENGLISH

POP3 (Post Office Protocol Version 3)   A set of software protocols or rules used to download mail to your computer. Your e-mail resides on the POP3 server until you connect and download it to your computer.

- **IMAP**—IMAP is a protocol that allows Outlook to download e-mail from an IMAP mail server. IMAP differs from POP3 in that your e-mail is not removed from the mail server when you connect to the server with your e-mail client (Outlook). Instead, you are provided a list of saved and new messages, which you can then open and read. IMAP is particularly useful when one e-mail account may be accessed by more than one computer, allowing the messages to be available from more than one computer.

  You might think that IMAP is a good idea because it leaves the e-mail on the mail server. However, you can use IMAP only if your ISP or company provides an IMAP mail server. In most cases, ISPs don't want your mail on their server, so they use POP3, which sends the mail to your computer when you connect.

PLAIN ENGLISH

IMAP (Internet Message Access Protocol)   A set of software rules used by an e-mail client to access e-mail messages on a shared mail server as if the messages were stored locally.

- **HTTP**—The Hypertext Transfer Protocol is the protocol and set of rules that enables you to browse Web sites using a Web browser. HTTP e-mail is accessed through a Web site, and your inbox actually resides on a server that is hosted by the provider of the e-mail Web site. Common providers of this type of e-mail include Microsoft (in the case of Hotmail) and Yahoo! (in the case of Yahoo! mail). Normally, such e-mail is accessed from the provider's Web site; however, Outlook can be configured to act as your e-mail client with HTTP mail providers.

- **Additional Server Types**—This selection allows you to configure Outlook as a mail client for other e-mail server types, such as Microsoft Mail or third-party e-mail server software. It also provides you with the capability to create a special e-mail account that allows you to receive faxes in the Outlook Inbox.

Even though Outlook pretty much demands that you configure an e-mail account during the initial Outlook setup, it doesn't easily provide for the fact that you might want to set up more than one account. However, it is very easy to add additional e-mail accounts as needed, which is discussed later in this lesson. The two most common uses for Outlook are as a Microsoft Exchange Server e-mail client or as an Internet e-mail client using POP3, IMAP, or HTTP. In the following sections, you take a closer look at the configuration steps for setting up your first POP3 or HTTP account. You can then learn how to add additional accounts after Outlook has been initially configured.

TIP

Importing E-mail Settings   If you are already using an e-mail client, such as Outlook Express, you can import all the e-mail messages and the settings for your e-mail accounts into Outlook. Outlook actually prompts you to perform this import when you start it for the first time. If you import mail settings, you won't be required to add an e-mail account as outlined in this section. You can use the information in this lesson, however, to add any additional e-mail accounts that you might need.

INTERNET POP3 E-MAIL

If you connect to the Internet using a modem, a DSL router, or a broadband cable modem, your Internet connection is of the type that an Internet service provider (ISP) provides. Most ISPs provide e-mail to their users in the form of a POP3 account. This means that the ISP's e-mail server holds your e-mail until you connect and download your messages to Outlook.

 **PLAIN ENGLISH**

> **ISP (Internet Service Provider)**   A commercial, educational, or government institution that provides individuals and companies access to the Internet.

ISPs that provide e-mail service also must have some mechanism for you to send e-mail to other users on the Internet. A computer called an SMTP server handles the sending of e-mail from your computer, over the Internet, to a final destination. That destination is typically the POP3 server that serves as the mail drop for the person to whom you are sending the Internet e-mail.

PLAIN ENGLISH

> **SMTP (Simple Mail Transfer Protocol)**   A set of rules used to transfer Internet mail; your ISP goes through an SMTP host, or relay, server to get your mail to you.

If you do not use an e-mail account (such as a POP3 account) that your ISP supplies to you, you can still use Outlook for Internet e-mail. In this case, sign up for an HTTP e-mail account on the Web and configure Outlook to use it. Configuring HTTP e-mail is discussed in a moment, but first take a look at the steps required to configure a POP3 e-mail account as Outlook's initial e-mail account.

The first thing Outlook needs you to provide is information related to the POP3 account, such as your username, password, and SMTP and

POP3 servers, all of which your ISP must provide. To complete the configuration of your POP3 account, follow these steps:

1. Select the **POP3** button on the E-mail Accounts screen, and then click **Next** to continue.

2. On the next screen, shown in Figure 3.3, enter your name, your e-mail address, your username, and your password. You also must provide the name of your ISP's POP3 (incoming server) and SMTP server (outgoing server) in the appropriate box. If your ISP uses Secure Password Authentication, which provides a second layer of authentication for their mail servers, click the Log on using Secure Password Authentication (SPA). (If SPA is used, you are provided a second username and password, other than your e-mail user-name, to log onto the servers; most ISPs do not use SPA.)

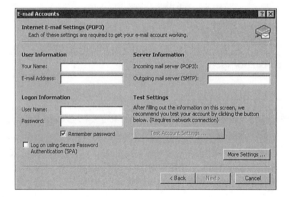

FIGURE 3.3
You must supply all the information listed on the Internet E-mail Settings (POP3) screen.

3. You can test your new account settings to make sure that they work; be sure you are connected to the Internet, and then click the **Test Account Settings** button. Outlook tests the user account and the servers listed. A Test Account Settings

dialog box appears, as shown in Figure 3.4. To close the dialog box, click **Close**.

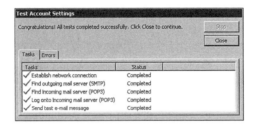

FIGURE 3.4
You can check your Internet e-mail settings after entering the appropriate information.

4. When you have completed your POP3 configuration settings (and tested them), click the **Next** button.

5. A final screen appears, letting you know that you have provided all the necessary information. Click **Finish** to end the process and open the Outlook Inbox.

PLAIN ENGLISH

Configuring for IMAP   The steps to configure an IMAP account are the same as those listed to configure the POP3 Internet e-mail account. The only differences are that you select IMAP on the initial setup screen and then make sure that the IMAP server name is provided on the configuration screen rather than the POP3 server name.

HTTP E-MAIL ACCOUNTS

Although most people use either an Exchange Server (configured by a system administrator) or a POP3 account as their primary e-mail account, Web-based HTTP accounts, such as Microsoft Hotmail, are convenient for checking personal e-mail from any computer.

Typically, you must log on to the appropriate Web site and provide a username and password to access your HTTP e-mail account. Although this offers a degree of flexibility that is appealing to many users, others are often put off because, in the past, this has prevented them from checking their e-mail using Outlook.

Fortunately, Outlook now has the capability to access HTTP e-mail accounts directly from Outlook. Before you can configure the HTTP account, however, you must sign up for an account on the site of HTTP mail service provider that you want to use. Assuming that you have an active account, follow these steps to configure an HTTP e-mail account:

1. Rather than selecting POP3, as you did in the previous section, select the **HTTP** option button on the E-mail Accounts dialog box (shown previously in Figure 3.2). Click **Next** to continue.

2. On the next screen, shown in Figure 3.5, enter your name, your e-mail address, your username, and your password (supplied by your mail provider). If you use an HTTP provider other than Hotmail, select **Other** in the HTTP Mail Service Provider dialog box, and then provide the URL of your HTTP service (you are providing the Web page address of the service).

3. Click **Next** after entering all the necessary information. On the final screen that appears, click **Finish**.

You are then returned to the Outlook window. When you add an HTTP account, such as a Hotmail account, to Outlook, a second set of folders appears in the Outlook folder listings, including Deleted Items, Inbox, Outbox, and Sent Items. Figure 3.6 shows this new set of folders.

Because a second set of folders is created, you can access the HTTP account from Outlook, but you manage received, sent, or deleted mail in their own set of folders. Mail received on any other accounts you might have, such as a POP3 account, are still located in your main Outlook Inbox.

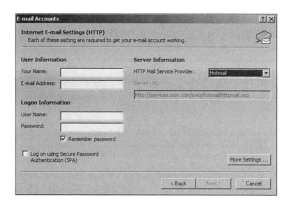

FIGURE 3.5
You must supply all the information listed on the HTTP E-mail Settings screen.

FIGURE 3.6
The HTTP mail folders, such as Hotmail, appear in the Outlook Folders list.

ADDING OTHER TYPES OF E-MAIL ACCOUNTS

As previously mentioned, Outlook is typically used as an e-mail client for either Exchange Server environments or for Internet e-mail where an ISP supplies either a POP3, an IMAP, or an HTTP e-mail account. However, many users find that they have more than one type of account at their disposal. Very often, users get one or more accounts through their ISP, but also sign up for an HTTP account that they can have easy access to from multiple locations (these HTTP accounts are usually free).

 TIP

Configuring Exchange Server E-mail Accounts   If you are using Outlook on a corporate network that uses an Exchange Server as the e-mail server, your account will typically be set up on your computer by the network administrator. The name of the Exchange Server and your network user name are required to complete the configuration. If you use Outlook on a corporate network, consult your network administrator for help in configuring Outlook. Using Outlook for e-mail on an Exchange Server network enables several e-mail features that are not available when you use Outlook for Internet e-mail, such as a POP3 account. On a network, you can redirect replies, set message expirations, and even grant privileges to other users who can then monitor your e-mail, calendar, contacts, and tasks.

You can use the following steps to add e-mail accounts to the Outlook settings after you have already made your initial configuration, as discussed in the previous sections of this lesson. Remember, you can add any type of e-mail account to Outlook after the fact.

In the Outlook window:

1. Select **Tools, E-mail Accounts**. The E-mail Accounts dialog box opens, as shown in Figure 3.7.

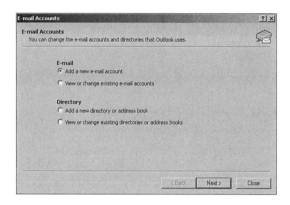

FIGURE 3.7
E-mail accounts are added using the E-mail Accounts dialog box.

2. Select the **Add a New E-mail Account** option button, and click **Next** to continue.

3. The Server Type screen opens with a list of the different types of e-mail accounts (this is the same screen provided during the initial e-mail configuration for Outlook, shown earlier in Figure 3.2).

4. Select the type of e-mail account you want to add to the Outlook configuration, and then click the **Next** button.

The information needed to configure a particular e-mail type is requested on the next screen, as previously discussed in this lesson.

DELETING E-MAIL ACCOUNTS

As you've seen in this lesson, configuring Outlook with different types of e-mail accounts is a pretty straightforward process. You might also find, on occasion, that you want to delete an e-mail account from the Outlook configuration. To do so, follow these steps:

1. Select **Tools, E-mail Accounts**. In the E-mail Accounts dialog box, select the **View or Change Existing E-mail Accounts** option button, and then click **Next**.

2. The E-mail Accounts dialog box appears as shown in Figure 3.8. To delete an account, select the account, and then click the **Remove** button.

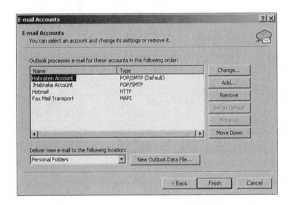

FIGURE 3.8
E-mail accounts are managed in the E-mail Accounts dialog box.

3. You are asked to confirm the deletion of the account. Click **Yes** to continue.

You can also use the E-mail Accounts dialog box to edit the settings for any of the e-mail accounts that you have created. Select the appropriate account, and then select the **Change** button. A dialog box for that specific account opens as shown in Figure 3.9, and you can change settings as required.

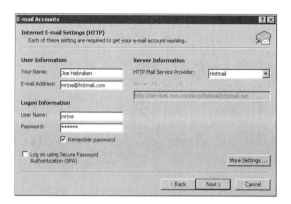

FIGURE 3.9
E-mail accounts settings can be edited using their settings dialog box.

In some cases, you might need to configure special settings for an e-mail account, such as how your computer connects to the Internet when you are using a particular e-mail account. Select the **More Settings** button on the e-mail accounts settings dialog box. The E-mail Settings dialog box appears for the e-mail account (see Figure 3.10).

The E-mail Settings dialog box has a series of tabs that differ depending on the type of e-mail account you are editing. In most cases (unless your ISP has provided you with special settings information), the only settings you will want to adjust are on the Connection tab, which allows you to specify how Outlook connects to the Internet when you are checking this particular account for e-mail.

After completing the addition of any special settings to the E-mail Settings dialog box, click **OK** to close it. You are returned to the dialog box for the e-mail account. Click **Next** to return to the E-mail Accounts dialog box, and then click **Finish** to return to Outlook.

In this lesson, you learned how to configure the initial Outlook e-mail account and how to add additional accounts. You also learned how to delete e-mail accounts from the Outlook configuration. In the next lesson, you will learn how to use the various Outlook tools, such as the Outlook bar.

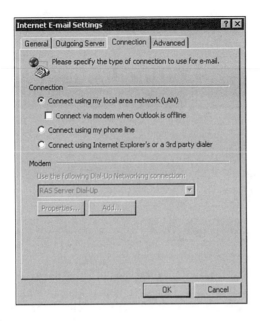

FIGURE 3.10
Special settings related to an e-mail account can be reached by clicking the More Settings button.

LESSON 4

Using Outlook's Tools

In this lesson, you learn how to change views in Outlook, how to use the Outlook bar, and how to use the Folder list.

USING THE OUTLOOK BAR

Each Outlook organizational tool has its own folder. You have a folder for e-mail (Inbox), a folder for the calendar (Calendar), and so on. The Outlook bar is a tool you can use to quickly change folders in Outlook. The icons in the Outlook bar represent all the folders available to you and provide shortcuts to getting to the contents of those folders. Figure 4.1 shows the Outlook bar and other areas of the Outlook window.

Three shortcut groups are located within the Outlook bar: Outlook Shortcuts, My Shortcuts, and Other Shortcuts. Each group contains related folders in which you can work.

- **Outlook Shortcuts**—This group contains folders for working with the different organizational tools in Outlook, such as Inbox, Calendar, Tasks, and so on.

- **My Shortcuts**—This group contains folders for organizing and managing e-mail you compose and send, such as the Outbox and the Sent Items folder. This group also provides access to the Journal (which keeps track of Office documents that you open and e-mail that you send) and an icon that takes you online to the Outlook Update Web page.

- **Other Shortcuts**—This group contains folders on your computer, such as My Computer, My Documents, and Favorites, which is a list of your favorite Web sites. You can use each of these folders to work with files and folders outside Outlook.

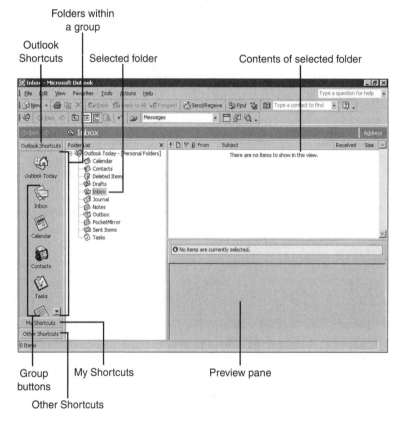

Folders within a group

Outlook Shortcuts

Selected folder

Contents of selected folder

Group buttons

My Shortcuts

Preview pane

Other Shortcuts

FIGURE 4.1
Use the Outlook bar to view various items in your work.

To switch from one group to another, click the **Outlook Shortcuts**, **My Shortcuts**, or **Other Shortcuts** button on the Outlook bar. The

Outlook shortcuts group is displayed by default, providing you with
quick access to tools such as your Inbox, Calendar, and Contacts list.

THE OUTLOOK SHORTCUTS FOLDERS

The Outlook Shortcuts group's folder icons in the Outlook bar enable
you to access your work in Outlook. That includes your e-mail messages, appointments, contact list, and so on. Table 4.1 describes each
of the folders within the Outlook Shortcuts group.

TABLE 4.1 Outlook Shortcuts Group Folders

Folder	Description
Outlook Today	Although not really a folder, the Outlook Today icon on the Outlook bar provides a summary of Calendar events, tasks, and new messages for the current day (today).
Inbox	Includes messages you've received by e-mail and fax.
Calendar	Contains your appointments, events, scheduled meetings, and so on.
Contacts	Lists names and addresses of the people with whom you communicate.
Tasks	Includes any tasks you have on your to-do list.
Notes	Lists notes you write to yourself or others.
Deleted Items	Includes any items you've deleted from other folders.

THE MY SHORTCUTS FOLDERS

The My Shortcuts group folders provide a method of organizing your
incoming and outgoing e-mail messages (see Figure 4.2). Table 4.2
describes each folder in the Mail group.

TABLE 4.2   My Shortcuts Folders

Folder	Description
Draft	Contains messages you have started but not sent.
Sent Items	Stores all messages you've sent.
Outbox	Contains messages to be sent.
Journal	Keeps track of your activities in Outlook, such as the logging of e-mail sent to specific contacts. The Journal also can keep track of your activities in other Office applications, such as Word or Excel.

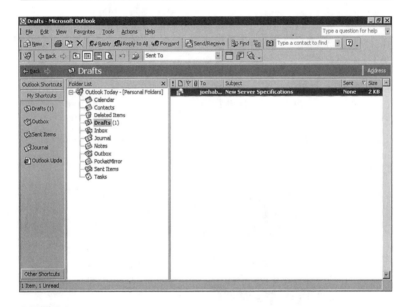

FIGURE 4.2
The My Shortcuts folder icons give you access to your e-mail and fax messages that have been saved as drafts, that have been sent, or that are waiting to be sent.

CAUTION

I See Other Folders in My Groups   You can add additional folders and folder icons very easily to Outlook. If you find folders other than the ones described here, folders have probably been added to your particular installation of Outlook.

THE OTHER SHORTCUTS FOLDERS

The Other Shortcuts group contains folders that are on your computer but not within Outlook: My Computer, My Documents, and Favorites. You can access a document or information in any of those areas so that you can attach it to a message, add notes to it, or otherwise use it in Outlook.

For example, with My Computer, you can view the contents of both hard and floppy disks, CD-ROM drives, and so on (see Figure 4.3). Double-click a drive in the window to view its folders and files. Double-click a folder to view its contents as well. Then, you can attach files to messages or otherwise use the files on your hard drive with the Outlook features.

KEEPING TRACK

Moving Up a Level   Use the **Back** button on the Advanced toolbar (right-click the Outlook toolbar and select **Advanced** on the shortcut menu) to return to a folder or drive after you've double-clicked to expand it and view its contents.

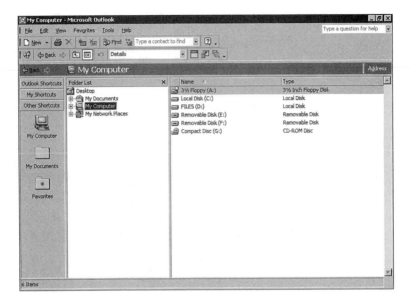

FIGURE 4.3
View your entire system through the My Computer folder in Outlook.

Using the Folder List

Outlook provides another method of viewing the folders within Outlook and your system: the Folder List. The Folder List displays the folders within any of the three groups (Outlook Shortcuts, My Shortcuts, or Other Shortcuts). From the list, you can select the folder you want to view.

To use the Folder List, first select the group (such as Outlook Shortcuts or Other Shortcuts) that contains the folders you want to view, and then select a particular folder (using the appropriate shortcut) from the Outlook bar to display the list (see Figure 4.4).

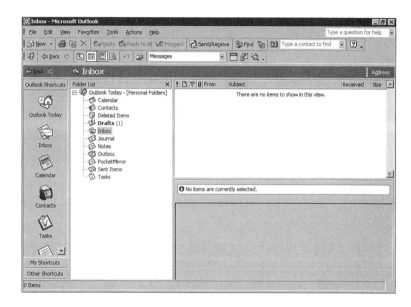

FIGURE 4.4
The Folder List shows all folders in the group you selected.

TIP

Pinning Down the Folder List   When you open the Folder List button on a particular folder's name, the Folder List floats on top of the current folder window. Click the **Push Pin** button in the upper-right corner of the Folder List to pin down the list in the Outlook window. If you want to close the Folder List, click its **Close** (**x**) button.

Choose any folder from the list, and the Information Viewer changes to reflect your selection. If you want to display another folder in the Information screen, click the folder to display its contents.

Changing Views

In Outlook, you are provided with different views that enable you to look at the information in your various folders from a particular perspective. Each view presents the information in a different format and organizational structure.

The easiest way to select the different views provided for each of your Outlook folders is to use a Current View drop-down box that is present on the Advanced toolbar for each folder type (Inbox, Calendar, Contacts, and so on). To open the Advanced toolbar (it doesn't matter which Outlook folder you currently have selected), follow these steps:

1. Point to the Standard toolbar for an Outlook folder (such as the Inbox) and click the right mouse button.

2. A shortcut menu appears, as shown in Figure 4.5. Click **Advanced**. The Advanced toolbar appears.

FIGURE 4.5
Right-click the Standard toolbar to access the Outlook Advanced toolbar.

3. If you find later that you would like to close the Advanced toolbar, repeat steps 1 and 2 to remove the check mark next to Advanced on the shortcut menu that appears.

TIP

You Must Open the Advanced Toolbar Only Once   After you've opened the Advanced toolbar for a folder, such as the Calendar or Inbox, it will be available for all the other Outlook folders.

Each folder, such as the Inbox, Calendar, Contacts, and so on, has a different set of buttons on the Standard and Advanced toolbars. This is because the commands and features that you access on a toolbar are particular to the folder that you currently have selected.

After you have the Advanced toolbar open, you can change the current view of any folder by clicking the **Current View** drop-down box, as shown in Figure 4.6. Each Current View box contains views that are appropriate for the currently selected folder on the Outlook bar.

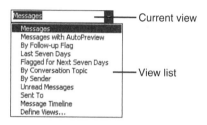

Current view

View list

FIGURE 4.6
Select a view to change the format of the information.

As you can see in Figure 4.6, you can change your view of the Inbox so that you can see the following:

- **Messages**—All messages

- **Messages with AutoPreview**—Messages and their first three lines of text

- **By Follow-Up Flag**—Messages that have been tagged with a follow-up flag

- **Last Seven Days**—Messages from the last seven days

- **Flagged for Next Seven Days**—Messages tagged with a flag for the next seven days

- **By Conversation Topic**—Messages organized by topic

- **By Sender**—Messages organized by sender

- **Unread Messages**—Unread messages only

- **Sent To**—Messages by recipient

- **Message Timeline**—Messages arranged in a timeline

Similarly, the Calendar folder, which is arranged in the Day/Week/ Month view type by default, enables you to view your appointments and events by Active Appointments, Day/Week/Month with Auto-Preview, Events, Recurring Appointments, and several other view types.

You can also change the view type for any of your folders by selecting the **View** menu and then pointing at **Current View**. The View list appears at the top of the Current View submenu.

As you work your way through the Outlook part of this book, you'll see examples of some of the different view types as they are used when you are working in Outlook. When you change folders in Outlook, take a quick look at the available views in the Current View drop-down list.

CREATING CUSTOM VIEWS

In addition to Outlook's many presupplied views, you can also create custom views of the information in your Outlook folders. To create a custom view for one of your Outlook folders, follow these steps:

1. Click the **View** menu and then point at **Current View**. Select **Define Views** (near the bottom of the Current View submenu). A Define Views dialog box for the currently selected folder opens.

2. Click the **New** button in the Define Views box. The Create a New View dialog box appears, as shown in Figure 4.7.

FIGURE 4.7
You can create custom views for your Outlook folders.

3. Enter a name for your new view and select a view type from the list in the Type of View box.

You can select different view types for a custom view:

- **Table**—Presents items in a grid of sorts in rows and columns. Use this view type to view mail messages, tasks, and details about any item.

- **Timeline**—Displays items as icons arranged in chronological order from left to right on a time scale. Use this to view journal entries and other items in this type of view.

- **Card**—Presents items such as cards in a card file. Use this to view contacts.

- **Day/Week/Month**—Displays items in a calendar view in blocks of time. Use this type for meetings and scheduled tasks.

- **Icon**—Provides graphical icons to represent tasks, notes, calendars, and so on.

4. After you've selected the type of view you want to create, click the **OK** button. A View Settings dialog box appears

based on your selection. In this box, you determine which
fields you want to have in the view and the fonts and other
view settings you want to use.

5. After you've selected the fields and view settings, click
Apply View. The items in the current folder appear in the
new view.

TIP

Using the Create a New View Option Buttons   If you
work on a network where Outlook folders are shared on
an Exchange Server, you can create your new view so
that you see only the information in the view. Alternatively, you can share the view with other users that
access the information. The default option in the Create
a New View dialog box is **This folder, visible to everyone**.
To reserve the custom view for yourself, click the **This
folder, visible only to me** option button. If you want to
use the new view for all your mail folders, click the **All
Mail and Post folders** option button.

PLAIN ENGLISH

Fields   A specific type of information that you want to
appear in your custom view. For a custom Inbox view
using the Timeline view type, the fields include
Received (when the message was received), Created
(when the message was created), and Sent (when the
message was sent).

Your newly created view appears on the Current View list on the
Advanced toolbar. You can select it by clicking the list's drop-down
arrow and then clicking the custom view's name.

CAUTION

Should I Design My Own Views?   Designing your own views can be complicated. Outlook provides several views for each folder on the Outlook bar. You might want to explore all these possibilities before you begin to create your own views.

USING OUTLOOK TODAY

Outlook Today is a great way to get a snapshot view of your day. This feature provides a window that lists all your messages, appointments, and tasks associated with the current day.

To open the Outlook Today window, click the **Go** menu and select **Outlook Today**. Icons for your Calendar, Messages, and Tasks appear in the Outlook Today window, as shown in Figure 4.8. Items for the current day are listed below the icons.

You can click any of the listed items (a particular appointment or task) to open the appropriate folder and view the details associated with the items. You can even update the items.

The Outlook Today Standard toolbar also provides a Type a Contact to Find box that you can use to quickly find people in your Contacts folder. Type a name into the Type a Contact to Find box (on the left of the Standard toolbar) and then press **Enter**. A Contact window appears for the person. You can edit the person's information or close the Contact box by clicking the **Close** button.

After you have viewed the items in the Outlook Today window, you can return to any of your folders by clicking their icons on the Outlook bar. Outlook Today is an excellent way to get a handle on what your day has in store for you.

In this lesson, you learned to use the Outlook Bar, change and create views in Outlook, use the Folder List, and take advantage of the Outlook Today feature. In the next lesson, you will learn to get help in Outlook.

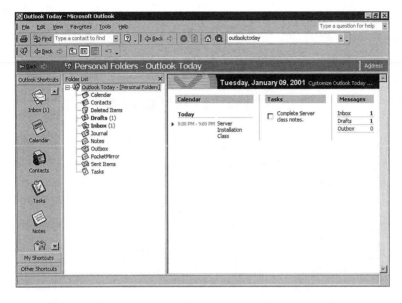

FIGURE 4.8
Outlook Today provides a list of all the items associated with the current day.

Lesson 5
Getting Help in Microsoft Outlook

In this lesson, you learn how to access and use the Help system in Microsoft Outlook.

Help: What's Available?

Microsoft Outlook supplies a Help system that makes it easy for you to look up information on Outlook commands and features as you compose e-mail messages and work with other Outlook features such as the Contacts list and the Calendar. Because every person is different, the Help system can be accessed in several ways. You can

- Ask a question in the Ask a Question box.
- Ask the Office Assistant for help.
- Get help on a particular element you see onscreen with the What's This? tool.
- Use the Contents, Answer Wizard, and Index tabs in the Help window to get help.
- Access the Office on the Web feature to view Web pages containing help information (if you are connected to the Internet).

USING THE ASK A QUESTION BOX

The Ask a Question box is a new way to access the Outlook Help system. It is also the easiest way to quickly get help. An Ask a Question box resides at the top right of the Outlook window.

For example, if you are working in Outlook and wish to view information on how to create a new appointment, type `How do I schedule a meeting?` into the Ask a Question box. Then press the **Enter** key. A shortcut menu appears below the Ask a Question box, as shown in Figure 5.1.

FIGURE 5.1
The Ask a Question box provides a list of Help topics that you can quickly access.

To access one of the Help topics supplied on the shortcut menu, click that particular topic. The Help window opens with topical matches for that keyword or phrase displayed.

In the case of the "meeting" question used in Figure 5.1, you could select **Schedule a meeting** from the shortcut menu that appears. This opens the help window and displays help on how to create a meeting (see Figure 5.2).

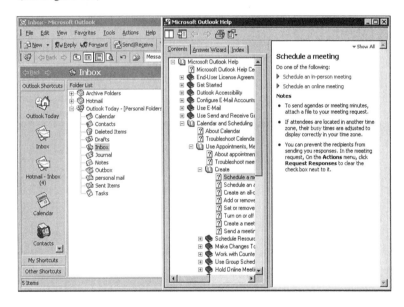

FIGURE 5.2
The Ask a Question box provides a quick way to access the Help window.

In the Help window, you can use the links provided to navigate the Help system. You can also use the Contents, Answer Wizard, and Index tabs to find additional information or look for new information in the Help window. You learn more about these different Help window tabs later in this lesson.

USING THE OFFICE ASSISTANT

Another way to get help in Outlook is to use the Office Assistant. The Office Assistant supplies the same type of access to the Help system as the Ask a Question box. You ask the Office Assistant a question, and it supplies you with a list of possible answers that provide links to various Help topics. The next two sections discuss how to use the Office Assistant.

TURNING THE OFFICE ASSISTANT ON AND OFF

By default, the Office Assistant is off. To show the Office Assistant in your application window, select the **Help** menu and then select **Show the Office Assistant**.

You can also quickly hide the Office Assistant if you no longer want it in your application window. Right-click the Office Assistant and select **Hide**. If you want to get rid of the Office Assistant completely so it isn't activated when you select the Help feature, right-click the **Office Assistant** and select **Options**. Clear the **Use the Office Assistant** check box, and then click **OK**. You can always get the Office Assistant back by selecting **Help, Show Office Assistant**.

ASKING THE OFFICE ASSISTANT A QUESTION

When you click the Office Assistant, a balloon appears above it. Type a question into the text box. For example, you might type **How do I print?** for help printing your work. Click the **Search** button.

The Office Assistant provides some topics that reference Help topics in the Help system. Click the option that best describes what you're trying to do. The Help window appears, containing more detailed information. Use the Help window to get the exact information that you need.

Although not everyone likes the Office Assistant because having it enabled means that it is always sitting in your Outlook window, it can be useful at times. For example, when you access particular features in Outlook, the Office Assistant can automatically provide you with context-sensitive help on that particular feature. If you are brand new to Microsoft Outlook, you might want to use the Office Assistant to help you learn the various features that Outlook provides as you use them.

TIP

Select Your Own Office Assistant Several different Office Assistants are available in Microsoft Office. To select your favorite, click the Office Assistant and select the **Options** button. On the Office Assistant dialog box that appears, select the **Gallery** tab. Click the **Next** button repeatedly to see the different Office Assistants that are available. When you locate the assistant you want to use, click **OK**.

USING THE HELP WINDOW

You can also forgo either the Type a Question box or the Office Assistant and get your help directly from the Help window. To directly access the Help window, select **Help** and then **Microsoft Outlook Help**. You can also press the **F1** key to make the Help window appear.

The Help window provides two panes. The pane on the left provides three tabs: Contents, Answer Wizard, and Index. The right pane of the Help window provides either help subject matter or links to different Help topics. It functions a great deal like a Web browser window. You click a link to a particular body of information and that information appears in the right pane.

The first thing that you should do is maximize the Help window by clicking its **Maximize** button. This makes it easier to locate and read the information that the Help system provides (see Figure 5.3).

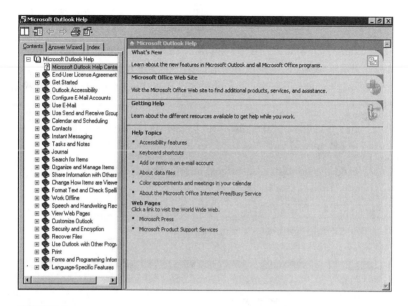

FIGURE 5.3
The Help window provides access to all the help information provided for Outlook.

When you first open the Help window, a group of links in the right pane provides you with access to information about new Outlook features and other links, such as a link to Microsoft's Office Web site. Next, take a look at how you can take advantage of different ways to find information in the Help window: the Contents tab, the Answer Wizard tab, and the Index tab.

TIP

View the Help Window Tabs   If you don't see the different tabs in the Help window, click the **Show** button on the Help window toolbar.

USING THE CONTENTS TAB

The Contents tab of the Help system is a series of books you can open. Each book has one or more Help topics in it, which appear as pages or chapters. To select a Help topic from the Contents tab, follow these steps:

1. In the Help window, click the **Contents** tab on the left side of the Help window.

2. Find the book that describes, in broad terms, the subject for which you need help.

3. Double-click the book, and a list of Help topics appears below the book, as shown in Figure 5.4.

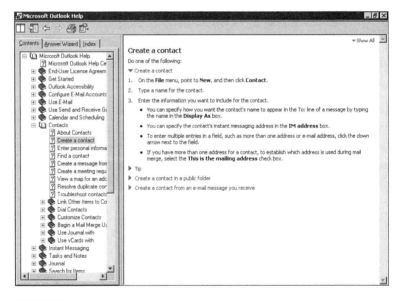

FIGURE 5.4

Use the Contents tab to browse through the various Help topics.

4. Click one of the pages (the pages contain a question mark) under a Help topic to display it in the right pane of the Help window.

5. When you finish reading a topic, select another topic on the Contents tab or click the Help window's **Close (x)** button to exit Help.

USING THE ANSWER WIZARD

Another way to get help in the Help window is to use the Answer Wizard. The Answer Wizard works the same as the Ask a Question box or the Office Assistant; you ask the wizard questions and it supplies you with a list of topics that relate to your question. You click one of the choices provided to view help in the Help window.

To get help using the Answer Wizard, follow these steps:

1. Click the **Answer Wizard** tab in the Help window.

2. Type your question into the What Would You Like to Do? box. For example, you might type the question, **How do I create a new contact?**

3. After typing your question, click the **Search** button. A list of topics appears in the Select Topic to Display box. Select a particular topic, and its information appears in the right pane of the Help window, as shown in Figure 5.5.

 TIP

> **Print Help**   If you want to print information provided in the Help window, click the **Print** icon on the Help toolbar.

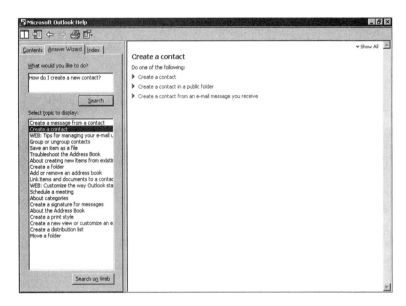

FIGURE 5.5
Search for help in the Help window using the Answer Wizard tab.

USING THE INDEX

The Index is an alphabetical listing of every Help topic available. It's like an index in a book.

Follow these steps to use the index:

1. In the Help window, click the **Index** tab.

2. Type the first few letters of the topic for which you are looking. The Or Choose Keywords box jumps quickly to a keyword that contains the characters you have typed.

3. Double-click the appropriate keyword in the keywords box. Topics for that keyword appear in the Choose a Topic box.

4. Click a topic to view help in the right pane of the Help window (see Figure 5.6).

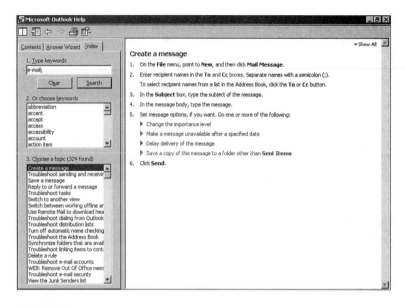

FIGURE 5.6
Use the Index tab to get help in the Help window.

TIP

> **Navigation Help Topics**   You can move from topic to topic in the right pane of the Help window by clicking the various links that are provided there. Some topics are collapsed. Click the triangle next to the topic to expand the topic and view the help provided.

GETTING HELP WITH SCREEN ELEMENTS

If you wonder about the function of a particular button or tool on the Outlook screen, wonder no more. Just follow these steps to learn about this part of Help:

1. Select **Help** and then **What's This?** or press **Shift+F1**. The mouse pointer changes to an arrow with a question mark.

2. Click the screen element for which you want help. A box
   appears explaining the element.

TIP

> **Take Advantage of ScreenTips**   Another Help feature
> provided by Outlook is the ScreenTip. All the buttons on
> the different toolbars provided by Outlook have a
> ScreenTip. Place the mouse on a particular button or
> icon, and the name of the item (which often helps you
> determine its function) appears in a ScreenTip.

In this lesson, you learned how to access the Outlook Help feature. In
the next lesson, you will learn how to create and send e-mail messages.

LESSON 6
Creating Mail

In this lesson, you learn how to compose a message, format text, check your spelling, and send e-mail. You also learn how to use different e-mail formats such as plain text and HTML.

COMPOSING A MESSAGE

You can send an e-mail message to anyone for whom you have an e-mail address, whether that address is in your list of contacts or scribbled on a Post-it note. In addition to sending a message to one or more recipients, in Outlook you can forward or copy messages to individuals in your Contacts list. You can even e-mail groups of people who are listed in your various distribution lists.

TIP

> **Compose Your Messages Offline**   If you connect to an Internet service provider and don't want to waste precious connect time while you compose e-mail messages, you can create new messages in Outlook without being connected to the Internet. New messages you send are placed in your Outbox until you connect to the Internet and actually send them on to their final destination. When you are connected to the Internet, all you have to do is click the **Send/Receive** button on the Standard toolbar (or **Tools**, **Send/Receive**, **Send All**) to send any messages held in the Outbox.

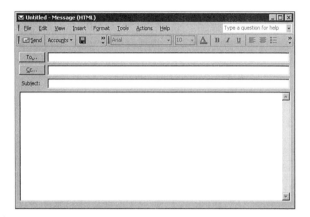 To open format the text of a new e-mail message while in the Outlook Inbox, select **File**, point at **New**, and then select **Mail Message** in the Outlook Inbox window. (You can also click the **New** button on the Standard toolbar.) A new message window appears (see Figure 6.1).

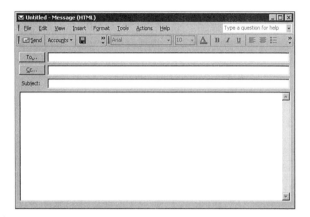

FIGURE 6.1
Compose a new message in the Untitled Message window.

E-mail addresses can be placed in the To box of a message that you want to send (a message you create from scratch or an existing message that you are forwarding) in several ways. You can

- Use your Outlook Contacts list.
- Use your Outlook Address Book.
- Type in an e-mail address that you don't currently have in any of your lists.

In the case of e-mail messages that you reply to, the e-mail address of the person who sent you the message is automatically placed in the To box, making it ready to be sent.

Having e-mail addresses listed in either your Contacts list or the Outlook Address Book is the easiest way to add an e-mail address to a list. It also helps you keep organized, and that is probably one of the reasons why you're using Outlook in the first place. You will also find that having e-mail addresses readily available in an Outlook list makes it easier to send carbon copies (duplicate e-mails) or blind carbon copies of messages when you are composing a particular message.

PLAIN ENGLISH

Blind Carbon Copy   A blind carbon copy (Bcc) of a message is a copy sent to someone in secret; the other recipients have no way of knowing that you are sending the message to someone as a blind carbon copy.

You can find more information on using Outlook's Personal Address Book in Lesson 12, "Using the Outlook Address Books." Lesson 13, "Creating a Contacts List," shows you how to use contacts.

To address a new e-mail message, follow these steps:

1. In the message window, click the **To** button to display the Select Names dialog box. Names that have been entered in your Contacts list appear on the left side of the dialog box. If you want to switch to a different list, such as the Outlook Address Book, click the drop-down list on the upper-right corner of the dialog box and make a new selection.

   If the e-mail address you want isn't in your Contacts list, instead of clicking the **To** button, type the e-mail address directly into the To text box (if you do this, you can then skip steps 3 through 7).

2. From the list of addresses that appears on the left of the dialog box, choose the name of the intended recipient and select the **To** button (or you can double-click the name). Outlook

copies the name to the Message Recipients list. You can also add any distribution lists to the To box that appear in your address list. To send a carbon copy or blind carbon copy to a recipient, use the **Cc** or **Bcc** buttons.

Figure 6.2 shows a message that is addressed to an individual whose address was contained in the Contacts list and also to a group of people who are listed in a distribution list (you can enter as many addresses as you want).

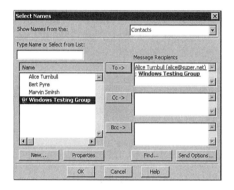

FIGURE 6.2
Add e-mail addresses or distribution list names quickly with the Select Names dialog box.

3. Click **OK** to return to the message window. Click in the Subject box and type the subject of your message.

4. Click in the text area, and then enter the text of the message. You do not have to press the Enter key at the end of a line; Outlook automatically wraps the text at the end of a line for you. You can use the Delete and Backspace keys to edit the text you enter.

5. When you finish typing the message, you can send the message, or you can format the message or check the spelling as detailed later in this lesson. To send the message, click the **Send** button on the message's Standard toolbar.

CAUTION

> **No Address**   If you try to send a message without enter-
> ing an address, Outlook displays a message that at least
> one e-mail address must be in the To box. Type in an
> address or select an address from your Contacts list or
> Address Book.

FORMATTING TEXT

You can enhance the format of the text in your message to make it
more attractive, to make it easier to read, or to add emphasis. Any formatting you do transfers to the recipient with the message if the recipient has Outlook or another e-mail client that can work with HTML or
Rich Text Format messages. However, if the recipient doesn't have an
e-mail client that can handle these special message formats, formatting might not transfer and the message will be received in plain text.

PLAIN ENGLISH

> **HTML**   Hypertext Markup Language is used to design
> Web pages for the World Wide Web. Outlook can send
> messages in this format, providing you with several text
> formatting options. Graphics can even be pasted into an
> HTML message.

PLAIN ENGLISH

> **Rich Text Format**   A special e-mail format developed by
> Microsoft for use with Microsoft mail systems. Outlook
> can send and receive messages in Rich Text Format.
> This enables you to send and receive messages with
> special formatting, such as bold, italic, various fonts,
> and other special characters and graphics.

You format text in two ways. You can format the text after you type it
by selecting it and then choosing a font, size, or other attribute; or you

can select the font, size, or other attribute to toggle it on, and then enter the text, which will be formatted as you type.

To format the text in your message, first make sure the Formatting toolbar is showing. On the menu system provided by the message window, select **View**, and then select **Toolbars** and click **Formatting**. Figure 6.3 shows a message with the Formatting toolbar displayed. Formatting options have also been applied to the text in the message. Table 6.1 explains the buttons found on the Formatting toolbar.

CAUTION

The Formatting Toolbar Buttons Don't Work   Only messages sent in HTML or Rich Text Format can be formatted. Plain-text messages don't supply you with any formatting options. So, even if the Formatting toolbar appears at the top of a plain-text message, the formatting options will not be available. Selecting the message type (such as HTML or plain text) is discussed in the section "Selecting the E-mail Message Format," found later in this lesson.

Formatting toolbar

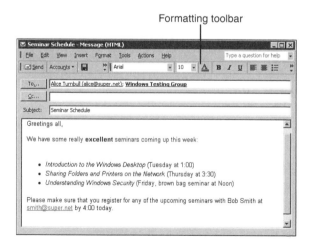

FIGURE 6.3
Use the Formatting toolbar to modify format of your message text.

TABLE 6.1   Formatting Toolbar Buttons

Button	Name
A	Font Color
B	Bold
I	Italic
U	Underlineformat of the text
≡	Align Left
≡	Center
≡	Align Right
⋮≡	Bullets
⋮≡	Numbering
⋶	Decrease Indent
⋶	Increase Indent
—	Insert Horizontal Line

CAUTION

My Toolbars Look Completely Different!   If you are using Microsoft Word as your e-mail editor, the toolbars that are present in the new message window reflect those you have selected in your Word installation. The Word and Outlook toolbars have many of the same buttons.

1. To apply a new font to format the selected text, on the Formatting toolbar, click the down arrow in the **Font** box. Scroll through the font list, if necessary, to view all fonts on the system, and then click the font you want to apply to the text. You can also apply a style to selected text in the message. On the Formatting toolbar, click the **Style** drop-down arrow. The styles available range from a set of predefined heading styles to special styles such as Numbered list and Bulleted list.

2. Assign a size by clicking the down arrow beside the **Font Size** drop-down list and choosing the size; alternatively, you can type a size into the Font Size text box.

3. To choose a color, click the **Color** button and select a color from the palette box that appears.

4. Choose a type style to apply to text by clicking the **Bold**, **Italic**, and/or **Underline** buttons on the Formatting toolbar.

5. Choose an alignment by selecting the **Align Left**, **Center**, or **Align Right** button from the Formatting toolbar.

6. Add bullets to a list by clicking the **Bullets** button on the Formatting toolbar. If you prefer a numbered list, click the **Numbering** button.

7. Create text indents or remove indents in half-inch increments by clicking the **Increase Indent** or **Decrease Indent** buttons. (Each time you click the Indent button, the indent changes by one-half inch.)

8. If you want to divide the text in the message using a horizontal line, place the insertion point at the appropriate place in the text and then click the **Add Horizontal Line** button.

TIP

Yuck, No Thanks! If you assign formatting to your text and don't particularly like it, click **Edit** and select **Undo** to remove the last formatting that you assigned.

SELECTING THE E-MAIL MESSAGE FORMAT

The default message format in Outlook is HTML. If you send most of your messages to individuals who don't have mail clients that can read the HTML format, you might want to change the default to plain text. On corporate networks, you might find an advantage to using the Rich Text Format as the default text format for your messages. This file format was developed for the Exchange Server mail environment used on most business networks.

The default format is set in the Outlook Options dialog box on the Mail Format tab. Fortunately, Outlook makes it very easy for you to switch the format of a mail message while you are composing the message. First, take a look at how to set the default mail type, and then look at how to change the message format while composing the message.

To set the default message format:

1. Click **Tools, Options**. The Options dialog box appears.

2. Click the **Mail Format** tab (see Figure 6.4).

TIP

Include Hyperlinks If you use the HTML or Rich Text Format message formats, you can include hyperlinks in your e-mails. Hyperlinks are Web addresses and e-mail addresses that can be accessed by clicking them in the message. Just type the Web address or e-mail address, and the hyperlink is created automatically in the message.

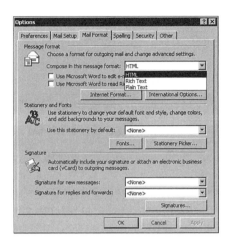

FIGURE 6.4
You can send your messages in HTML, Rich Text Format, or plain-text format.

3. To select the message format, click the **Compose in This Message Format** drop-down box. Select **HTML**, **Rich Text**, or **Plain Text**. If you want to use Microsoft Word as your e-mail editor, click the **Use Microsoft Word to Edit E-Mail Messages** check box.

PLAIN ENGLISH

Using HTML Stationery   If you use the HTML format for your messages, you can also select to use a particular stationery on the Mail Format tab. Stationery types can be previewed using the **Stationery Picker** button. Be advised that HTML stationery will slow down the loading of e-mail messages on the recipient's computer, and not everyone will have a mail client that can view the stationery. You probably should use the stationery only for personal messages to friends and family members who also use Outlook as their e-mail client.

CHECKING SPELLING

Because you don't want to look like you wedged a crayon in your brain during your childhood years, and you generally want to maintain your professional image, you should check the spelling in your mail messages before you send them. Outlook includes a spelling checker you can use for that purpose. If you are using Word as your e-mail editor, you will use the Word Spelling and Grammar features.

To check the spelling in a message, follow these steps:

1. In a message window, choose **Tools**, and then select **Spelling** or press **F7**. If the spelling checker finds a word whose spelling it questions, it displays the Spelling dialog box (shown in Figure 6.5). (If no words are misspelled, a dialog box appears saying that the spelling check is complete; choose **OK** to close the dialog box.)

FIGURE 6.5
Check your spelling before sending a message.

2. Your response to the word Outlook questions in the Spelling dialog box will vary. If you recognize that Outlook has correctly flagged a misspelled word, choose one of the following:

    *   **Suggestions**—Select the correct spelling in this text box, and it automatically appears in the Change To text box.

- **Change**—Click this button to change this particular occurrence of the word in question to the spelling in the Change To text box.

- **Change All**—Click this button to change the word in question to the spelling listed in the Change To text box every time the spelling checker finds the word in this message.

If Outlook checks a word that you know is already spelled correctly (such as a proper name), choose one of the following:

- **Not in Dictionary**—Enter the correct spelling into this text box.

- **Ignore**—Click this button to continue the spelling check without changing this occurrence of the selected word.

- **Ignore All**—Click this button to continue the spelling check without changing any occurrence of the word in question throughout this message.

- **Add**—Click this button to add the current spelling of the word in question to the dictionary so that Outlook will not question future occurrences of this spelling.

- **Undo Last**—Click this button to undo your last spelling change and return to that word.

3. Continue until the spelling check is complete (or click **Cancel** to quit the spelling check).

4. Outlook displays a message box telling you that the spell check is complete. Click **OK** to close the dialog box.

TIP

> **Set Your Spelling Options**   Click the **Options** button in the Spelling dialog box to set options that tell Outlook to do such things as ignore words with numbers, ignore original message text in forwarded messages or replies, always check spelling before sending, and so on.

ADD A SIGNATURE

You can further personalize your e-mails by adding a signature to the message. A signature can be as simple as just your name, or the signature can include your phone number or extension or other information. Some people even add a favorite quote to their signature. If you use HTML as your message format, you can even include signature files that contain graphics. Plain-text signatures (for use with plain-text messages) will consist only of text characters.

First, take a look at how you can create a signature. Then you can take a look at how you apply it to a message.

CREATING A SIGNATURE

1. Choose **Tools, Options** to open the Options dialog box, and then select the **Mail Format** tab.

2. Click the **Signatures** button at the bottom of the dialog box. The Create Signature dialog box opens.

3. Click the **New** button; the Create a New Signature dialog box opens as shown in Figure 6.6.

4. Type a name for your new signature, and then click **Next**.

5. The Edit Signature dialog box appears. Enter the text you want included in the signature. You can use the Paragraph or Font buttons to add formatting to the text in the signature.

6. When you have finished creating your signature, click the **Finish** button. Click **Close** to close the Create Signatures dialog box, and then click **OK** to close the Options dialog box.

FIGURE 6.6
Outlook walks you through the steps of creating a signature.

TIP

> **You Can Edit Signatures**   To edit a signature, select the signature in the Create Signatures dialog box and then click **Edit**.

INSERTING THE SIGNATURE

After you've created a signature or signatures, you can quickly add it to any message by placing the insertion point where you want to place the signature, choosing **Insert**, and then choosing **Signature**; all the signatures that you have created appear on the menu. Select the signature from the list you want to use in the message you are currently composing.

You can also preview the signatures before inserting them; choose **Insert**, **Signature**, and then select **More** from the cascading menu. The Select a Signature dialog box opens. Select any of your signatures to view a preview of the signature. When you find the signature you want to use, click **OK**.

Sending Mail

You probably know that after you add recipient addresses, compose your message, format the text, spell check the message, and insert a signature in the e-mail, you are ready to send the message. But you can use a couple of ways to actually send the message on its way.

The fastest way to send the message using the mouse is to click the Send button on the Message toolbar. If you prefer, press **Ctrl+Enter**. In either case, your message is heading out to its destination. If you are working offline, the message is placed in the Outbox until you connect to the Internet and send and receive your messages.

Recalling a Message

If you use Outlook as an e-mail client in a Microsoft Exchange Server environment, you can actually recall or replace e-mail messages that you have sent. But you can recall or replace only messages that have not been opened by the recipient or moved to another folder by a recipient.

If the Folder List is not visible, click the **View** menu, and then click **Folder List**.

1. Click the **My Shortcuts** button on the Outlook bar, and then select the **Sent Items** folder.

2. Double-click to open the message that you want to recall.

3. In the message window, click the **Actions** menu, and then click **Recall This Message**. The Recall This Message dialog box opens as shown in Figure 6.7.

4. To recall the message, click the **Delete Unread Copies of This Message** option button, and then click **OK**. A notice appears in the message window informing you that you attempted to recall this message on a particular date and at a particular time.

FIGURE 6.7
Messages that have not been read can be recalled or replaced.

5. If you want to replace the message with a new message, click the **Delete Unread Copies and Replace with New Message** option button. When you click **OK**, a new message window opens with a copy of the message you want to recall in it. Just change the message text or address and then send the message.

6. You eventually receive a notification in your Inbox (as new mail) notifying you whether the recall was successful.

In this lesson, you learned to compose a message, format text, check your spelling, and send mail. You also learned how to select different e-mail formats such as HTML and Plain Text and add a signature to an e-mail message. You also learned how to recall a message. In the next lesson, you will learn to work with received e-mail.

LESSON 7
Working with Received Mail

In this lesson, you learn how to read your mail, save an attachment, answer mail, and close a message.

READING MAIL

When you log on to Outlook, your Inbox folder appears, and any new messages you've received are downloaded from your ISP's (or your company's) mail server. If you use Internet mail and a dial-up connection (in contrast to DSL or cable modem connections, which are always connected), a dial-up connection must be made before Outlook can check the mail server for new mail.

No matter what the connection situation, after you download any new e-mail to your computer, the new mail appears in the Outlook Inbox (see Figure 7.1). If you watch closely when you connect to your network or Internet service provider, a downloading mail icon appears in the lower right of the Outlook window, showing you that new mail is being received.

As you can see in Figure 7.1, the Inbox provides important information about each message. For example, one message has been labeled as high priority and one message has an attachment. Messages that have already been replied to are marked with a curved reply arrow. You'll learn about file attachments in Lesson 9, "Attaching Files and Items to a Message," and mail priorities in Lesson 11, "Setting Mail Options."

Additional information about a particular message, such as the actual reply date, is contained at the top of the Preview pane when that particular message is selected. At the bottom of the Outlook status bar (on the left), information such as how many items are in the Inbox and how many message are unread is also provided.

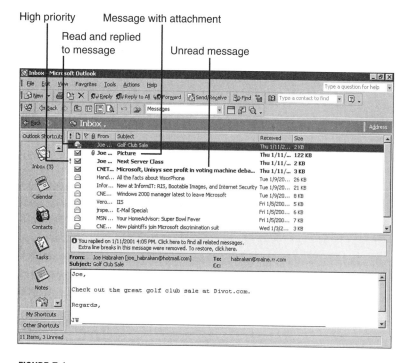

FIGURE 7.1
The Inbox provides information related to your received messages: the sender, the subject, the date received, and priority and attachment icons.

To read a message, you can select it, and its contents appear in the Outlook Preview pane. You can also open a message in its own window; double-click a mail message to open it. Figure 7.2 shows an open message.

To read the next or previous mail message in the Inbox when you have opened a mail message, click either the **Previous Item** or the **Next Item** button on the message window toolbar. To access more view choices, select the **View** menu, and then point at **Previous** or **Next**;

submenu choices are provided for each of these choices that allow you
to jump to another item, an unread item, or to a message that has been
assigned a particular priority or that has been flagged.

Previous Item   Next Item
button   button

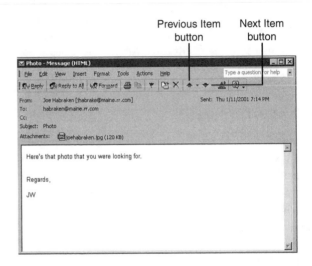

FIGURE 7.2
*The message window displays the message and tools for responding to the mes-
sage or moving to the previous or next message in the Inbox.*

PLAIN ENGLISH

> **Item**   Outlook uses the word *item* to describe a mail
> message, an attached file, an appointment or meeting, a
> task, and so on. Item is a generic term in Outlook that
> describes the currently selected element.

After you open a message in the Inbox, it is marked as read (notice
that the envelope that represents the message is opened). You can also
mark messages as read or unread by selecting **Edit** and then selecting
either **Mark As Read** or **Mark As Unread**. Additionally, you can
mark all the messages in the Inbox as read by choosing **Edit, Mark
All As Read**. You might want to mark mail messages as read so you
don't read them again; you might want to mark important mail as
unread so you'll be sure to open it and read it again.

TIP

 No Mail? Maybe Outlook is not configured to check for mail automatically. To force Outlook to look for mail, click the **Send and Receive** button on the toolbar, or choose **Tools**, point at **Send/Receive**, and then select **Send/Receive All**. Any new messages are placed in the Inbox.

SAVING AN ATTACHMENT

You often receive messages that have files or other items attached to them, such as graphical images. In the Inbox list of messages, an attachment is represented by a paper clip icon beside the message. Save any attachments sent to you so that you can open, modify, print, or otherwise use the attached document or image. Messages can contain multiple attachments.

CAUTION

What About Viruses? Unfortunately, there is a chance that an attachment to a message can be a virus or other malicious software. Computer viruses can really wreak havoc on your computer system. When you receive an e-mail message from someone you don't know and that message has an attachment, the best thing to do is delete the message without opening it or the attachment. Because viruses can read your address book and send themselves to the people it contains, even e-mail from known parties bears at least some scrutiny. If you save an attachment to your computer, you might want to check the file with an antivirus program before you actually open the file. Be especially cautious if the file that you receive as an attachment has an .exe or .vba extension. These extensions, which virus creators commonly use to get you to unleash a virus on your own computer, mark that the attachment is an actual program.

To save an attachment, follow these steps:

1. Open the message containing an attachment by double-clicking the message. The attachment appears as an icon below the subject area of the message (see Figure 7.3).

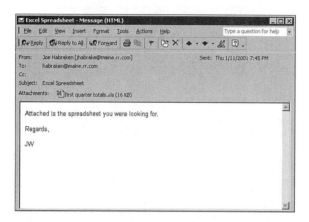

FIGURE 7.3
An icon represents the attached file.

2. (Optional) You can open the attachment from within the message by double-clicking the attachment icon. A message appears, as shown in Figure 7.4, warning you that attachments can contain viruses. To open the file, click the **Open It** option button and then click **OK**. The attachment will be opened in the application in which it was created (such as Word or Excel). When you have finished looking at the attachment, you can return to the e-mail message by closing the open application.

If you choose **Save the File to Disk**, a Save Attachment dialog box appears, allowing you to save the file to your hard drive.

3. You probably noticed in the Opening Mail Attachment message box that you also had the option to save the attachment (see Figure 7.4). There is another way to save your

attachments, and it actually makes it easier when you have to save multiple attachments attached to the same e-mail message. In the message window, select **File**, **Save Attachments**. The Save Attachment dialog box appears (see Figure 7.5).

FIGURE 7.4
You can open or save an attachment by double-clicking its icon.

FIGURE 7.5
Save the attachment to a convenient folder.

4. Choose the folder in which you want to save the attachment or attachments and click **Save**. The dialog box closes and returns to the message window. You can change the name of the file in the File Name box, if you want. After you save the

attachment, you can open the attachment, which is now like any other saved file on your computer, at any time from the application in which it was created.

TIP

> **Use the Right Mouse Button**   You can also quickly save an attachment by right-clicking the attachment icon. On the shortcut menu that appears, click **Save As**, and then save the attachment to an appropriate folder.

ANSWERING MAIL

You might want to reply to a message after you read it. The message window enables you to answer a message immediately, or at a later time if you prefer. To reply to any given message, follow these steps:

1. Select the message in the Inbox window, and then click the **Reply** button on the Inbox toolbar.

   If you have the message open, click the **Reply** button in the message window. The Reply message window appears, with the original message in the message text area and the sender of the message already filled in for you (see Figure 7.6).

TIP

> **Reply to All**   If you receive a message that has also been sent to others—as either a message or a carbon copy (Cc)—you can click the **Reply to All** button to send your reply to each person who received the message.

2. The insertion point is automatically placed above the message text that you are replying to. Enter your reply text.

3. When you finish your reply, click the **Send** button. Outlook sends the message.

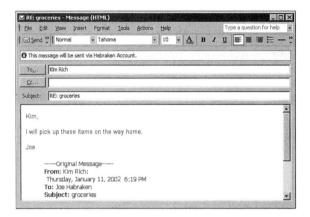

FIGURE 7.6
You can reply to a message quickly and easily.

The next time you open a message to which you've replied, there is a reminder at the top of the message window telling you the date and time you sent your reply. Don't forget that the purple arrow next to a message in the Inbox window shows that the message has been replied to.

PRINTING MAIL

You can print mail messages, either directly from the Inbox when they have been selected or from a message window when you have opened a particular message. To print an unopened message, select the message in the message list of the Inbox or other folder and choose **File**, **Print**. The Print dialog box opens; click **OK** to send the message to the printer. If the message is already open, you can follow these steps:

1. Open the message in Outlook.

2. Choose **File** and then select **Print**, or press **Ctrl+P** to view the Print dialog box.

3. In the Print dialog box, click **OK** to print one copy of the entire message using the printer's default settings. See Lesson

19, "Printing in Outlook," for detailed information about configuring pages and changing printer options.

TIP

> **Toolbar Shortcut**   Click the **Print** button on the tool-
> bar to print an unopened or opened message using the
> default print settings.

When you finish reading or printing a message, click the **Close** button
on the message window.

In this lesson, you learned to read your mail, save an attachment,
answer mail, and print a message. In the next lesson, you will learn
to delete and forward messages and create folders to store your
messages.

LESSON 8
Managing Mail

In this lesson, you learn how to delete and undelete messages, forward messages, and create folders. You also learn how to move messages to these folders.

DELETING MAIL

Although you might want to store certain important messages and perhaps even create folders to store them in, which is discussed in Lesson 10, "Saving Drafts and Organizing Messages," you'll definitely want to delete much of the mail that you receive after reading it. You can easily delete messages in Outlook when you're finished reading and sending replies to them.

 The easiest way to delete a selected message is to click the **Delete** button on the Outlook toolbar. If the message is open, just click the **Delete** button on the message window toolbar instead.

If you want to delete several messages in the Inbox, just select the messages using the mouse. To select several contiguous messages, click the first message, and then hold down the **Shift** key when you click the last message in the series. To select noncontiguous messages, hold down the **Ctrl** key and click each message. When you have all the messages selected that you want to delete, click the **Delete** button (or you can select the **Edit** menu and then select **Delete**).

UNDELETING ITEMS

If you change your mind and want to get back items you've deleted, you can usually retrieve them from the Deleted Items folder. By default, when you delete an item, it doesn't disappear from your computer; it merely moves to the Deleted Items folder. Items stay in the Deleted Items folder until you delete them from that folder—at which point they are unrecoverable. Typically, when you exit Outlook, the Deleted Items folder is emptied automatically. To retrieve a deleted item from the Deleted Items folder, follow these steps:

1. Click the scroll-down arrow on the Outlook bar to locate the Deleted Items folder.

2. Click the **Deleted Items** icon in the Outlook bar to open the folder.

3. Select the items you want to retrieve; you can then drag them back to the Inbox by dragging them and dropping them onto the Inbox icon in the Outlook bar. Or if you don't like dragging messages, select the files you want to move from the Deleted Items folder, and then select **Edit, Move to Folder**. The Move Items dialog box appears as shown in Figure 8.1.

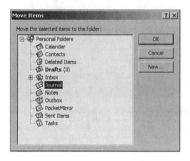

FIGURE 8.1
Deleted messages can be moved out of the Deleted Items folder back into the Inbox.

4. Select the folder you want to move the items into (such as the Inbox) and then click the **OK** button.

TIP

Use Undo Immediately   If you want to undelete a message or messages that you just deleted, select the **Edit** menu, and then select **Undo Delete.**

EMPTYING THE DELETED ITEMS FOLDER

If you're sure you want to delete the items in the Deleted Items folder, empty the contents of the folder. To delete items in the Deleted Items folder, follow these steps:

1. On the Outlook bar, choose **Outlook Shortcuts**, and then select the **Deleted Items** folder. All deleted items in that folder appear in the message list, as shown in Figure 8.2.

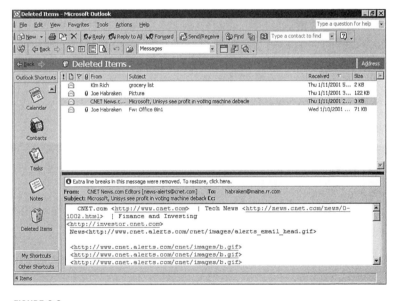

FIGURE 8.2
Deleted messages remain in the Deleted Items folder until you permanently delete them.

2. To permanently delete an item or items, select it (or them) in the Deleted Items folder.

3. Click the **Delete** button, or choose **Edit** and then select **Delete**. Outlook displays a confirmation dialog box asking whether you're sure you want to permanently delete the message. Choose **Yes** to delete the selected item.

4. To switch back to the Inbox or another folder, select the folder from either the Outlook bar or the Folder List.

 TIP

> **Automatic Permanent Delete**   You can set Outlook to permanently delete the contents of the Deleted Items folder every time you exit the program. To do so, in the Outlook window choose **Tools**, and then click **Options**. Select the **Other** tab of the Options dialog box and click the **Empty the Deleted Items Folder Upon Exiting** check box. Then click **OK**.

Forwarding Mail

You can forward mail that you receive to a co-worker or anyone else with an e-mail address. When you forward a message, you can also add comments to the messages if you so desire.

PLAIN ENGLISH

> **Forward Mail**   When you forward mail, you send a copy of a message you have received to another person; you can add your own comments to the forwarded mail, if you want.

You can forward an open message or a message selected in the message list in the Inbox in the same way. To forward mail, follow these steps:

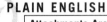 1. Select or open the message you want to forward. Then click the **Forward** button. The FW Message window appears (see Figure 8.3).

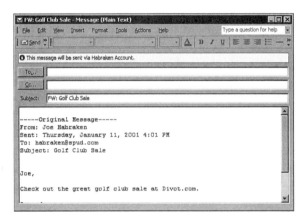

FIGURE 8.3
When you forward a message, the original message appears at the bottom of the message window.

2. In the To text box, enter the addresses of the people to whom you want to forward the mail. If you want to choose an address or addresses from a list, click the **To** button to display the Select Names dialog box, and then select the address or addresses from your Contacts list.

3. (Optional) In the Cc text box, enter the addresses of anyone to whom you want to forward copies of the message.

4. In the message area of the window, enter any message you want to send with the forwarded text.

PLAIN ENGLISH

Attachments Are Forwarded, Too   If the message that you forward contains attached files, the attachments are also forwarded.

5. When you are ready to send the message, click the **Send** button.

CREATING FOLDERS

Although Outlook provides you with an Inbox, an Outbox, a Sent Items folder, and a Deleted Items folder, you might find it advantageous to create your own folders. This provides you with alternative places to store items and can make finding them in the future easier (rather than just having all your messages languish in the Inbox). Folders can also be used to store items other than messages, so you could even create subfolders for your Contacts folder or Calendar.

TIP

Folders Aren't the Only Way to Get Organized   Although the creation of folders can help you organize messages and other items that you want to store in Outlook, another tool called the Organizer has been designed to help you move, delete, and even color code received e-mail messages. You will take a look at the Organizer in Lesson 10.

To create a folder, follow these steps:

1. Click the **Folder List** drop-down button , and then click the **Folder List pin** to "pin it down" to the Outlook window.

2. To create a folder in the Folder List, right-click the folder, such as the Inbox, that will serve as the parent folder for the new folder.

3. On the shortcut menu that appears (see Figure 8.4), select New Folder. The Create New Folder dialog box appears.

4. In the Create New Folder dialog box, type a name for the folder into the Name box.

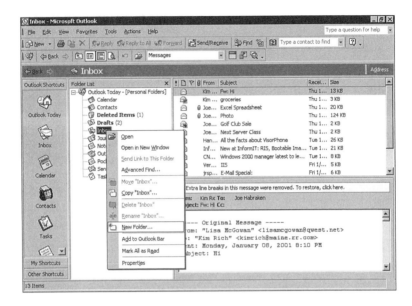

FIGURE 8.4
Folders can be created anywhere in the Folder List.

> **TIP**
>
> **Create Folders from the File Menu**   You can also open the Create New Folder dialog box from the File menu. Just select **File**, point at **New**, and then select **Folder**.

5. Use the icons in the New Folder dialog box main pane area to select the type of folder that you want to create. For example, if you want to hold mail messages in the folder, select the **Mail and Post** icon (see Figure 8.5).

6. Select the **Location** drop-down list to select the location for the new folder. If you want to nest the new folder in an existing folder, such as the Inbox, select that folder on the list. If you want to create the new folder as a first-level folder, select **Personal Folders**.

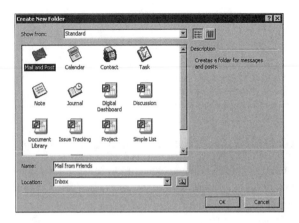

FIGURE 8.5
Folders can be created to hold mail messages, contacts, and even calendar appointments.

7. When you have finished making your entries and selections in the New Folder dialog box, click **OK** to create the folder.

8. You are asked whether you want to add a shortcut icon for the new folder to the Outlook bar. If you want to create the icon, click **Yes**.

The new folder appears on the Outlook bar and in the Folder List.

TIP

> **Add an Outlook Bar Shortcut for a Folder**   Even if you choose not to add a shortcut for the folder to the Outlook bar when you create the folder, you can add it later. Right-click any folder you've created in the Folder List and select **Add to Outlook Bar** from the shortcut menu that appears.

> **CAUTION**
>
> **I Want to Delete a Folder**   If you add a folder and then decide you don't want it, right-click the folder in the Folder List and select **Delete** from the shortcut menu. You then must verify the deletion; click **Yes**.

MOVING ITEMS TO ANOTHER FOLDER

You can move items from one folder in Outlook to another; for example, you can create a folder to store all messages pertaining to a specific account or just make a folder that holds personal messages instead of business-related messages. You can easily move any messages to a new folder and then open them later to read them or to reply to them.

To move an item to another folder, follow these steps:

1. From the Inbox or any Outlook folder, select the message or messages you want to move.

2. Select **Edit**, **Move to Folder**. The Move Items dialog box appears (see Figure 8.6).

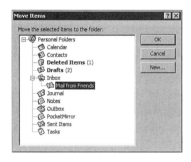

FIGURE 8.6

Choose the folder in which you want to store the message or messages.

3. In the Move Items dialog box, select the folder to which you want to move the message or messages.

4. Click **OK**. The message or messages are moved to the destination folder.

TIP

> **Quickly Move Items**   You can quickly move any message or other Outlook item by dragging it from the open folder in which it resides to any folder icon in the Outlook bar.

In this lesson, you learned to forward messages, delete messages, and create new folders and move items to those folders. In the next lesson, you will learn to attach files and other items to an e-mail message.

LESSON 9
Attaching Files and Items to a Message

In this lesson, you learn how to attach a file and Outlook items to an e-mail message.

ATTACHING A FILE

You can attach any type of file to an Outlook message, which makes for a convenient way of sending your files to your co-workers or sending pictures to family members across the country who use Internet e-mail. You can send Word documents, Excel spreadsheets, a family photo (taken from a digital camera or scanned from a photograph), or any other file you have on your hard drive.

When you attach a file, it appears as an icon in an attachment box that resides in the message window right below the Subject box, as shown in Figure 9.1. A button to the left of the attached file can be used to quickly access the Insert File dialog box if you want to change the attached file or add additional attachments before sending the message.

You can also open or view any files that you attach to your e-mail messages (before or after you send them) by double-clicking the file. Next, you take a look at attaching and viewing attachments, such as files created in other applications and picture files. Then, you can take a look at attaching an Outlook item such as a contact or appointment to an e-mail message.

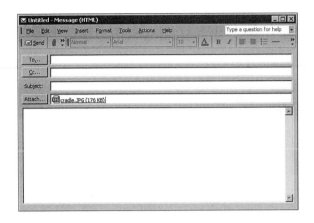

FIGURE 9.1
Attached files appear as icons in the Attach box.

To attach a file to a message, follow these steps:

1. In the new message window, choose Insert and then select File, or click the Insert File button on the toolbar. The Insert File dialog box appears (see Figure 9.2).

2. From the **Look In** drop-down list, choose the drive and folder that contain the file you want to attach.

3. Select the file you want to attach.

4. Click **OK** to insert the file into the message.

FIGURE 9.2
Select the file you want to attach to a message.

An Attach box appears below the Subject box on the message, and an icon and the filename are inserted.

PLAIN ENGLISH

Large Files Take Time   Sending an extremely large file can take a great deal of time, depending on your connection speed. Some ISPs, such as America Online, set a limit for attachment file size for sent or received attachments. Using tools that reduce the size of files—applications such as WinZip or Microsoft Compressed Folders—you can compress larger files. However, the recipient of a message in which you have included a "zipped" attachment needs the appropriate tool, such as WinZip, to uncompress the attached file.

ATTACHING OUTLOOK ITEMS

In addition to attaching files from other programs, you can also attach an Outlook item to a message. An Outlook item can be any item saved in one of your personal folders, including an appointment, a contact, a note, and so on. You can attach an Outlook item in the same manner you attach a file.

Follow these steps to attach an Outlook item:

1. In the message window, choose **Insert**, **Item**. The Insert Item dialog box appears (see Figure 9.3).

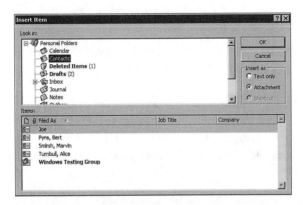

FIGURE 9.3
Select items from any folder in Outlook, such as a contact's information from the Contacts folder.

2. From the **Look In** list, choose the folder containing the item you want to include in the message.

3. Select from the items that appear in the **Items** list when you have the appropriate folder selected. To select multiple adjacent items, hold down the **Shift** key and click the first and last desired items; to select multiple nonadjacent items, hold down the **Ctrl** key and click the items.

4. In the Insert As area, choose from the following option buttons:

   • **Text Only**—Inserts the file as text into the message, such as the contact's information or the text in an e-mail message.

- **Attachment**—Attaches the e-mail message or Contact record as an attachment to the current e-mail message.

- **Shortcut**—If you are using Outlook in a networked environment where Exchange Server is used and all your folders, such as Contacts, are stored on the network, you can attach shortcuts to your e-mail message. Then, another user on the network can double-click the shortcut to access its information.

5. Click **OK**, and Outlook inserts the selected items into your message (either as an attachment or as inserted text).

Figure 9.4 shows an attached contact record in an Outlook e-mail message. When the e-mail recipient receives the message, he or she can access the contact information by double-clicking the attachment icon. The recipient can then save the contact information to their Contacts folder.

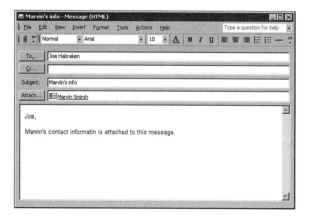

FIGURE 9.4
Select an item from any folder in Outlook, such as a contact's information, and attach it to your e-mail message.

PLAIN ENGLISH

It Doesn't Work Without Outlook   If recipients don't have Outlook on their computers, they will not be able to view the attached item, such as an Outlook contact record. If you know that a recipient doesn't have Outlook, insert the contact information into the message as text using the Text Only option in the Insert Item dialog box.

In this lesson, you learned how to attach files and Outlook items to an Outlook e-mail message. You also learned how to insert an object into an Outlook item. In the next lesson, you will learn to save draft messages and work with the Outlook Organizer.

LESSON 10
Saving Drafts and Organizing Messages

In this lesson, you learn how to save a draft, view messages that you've sent, and manage messages by creating rules using the Outlook Organizer.

SAVING A DRAFT

Suppose you start a message but you are called away or need to do something else before you can finish it. You don't have to lose the message by canceling, forcing you to start over again later; you can save the message in the Drafts folder and then open it later to complete it.

To save a draft, open and begin composing a new message. Then, follow these steps:

1. In the message window, click the **Close** button. A dialog box appears, asking whether you want to save changes, as shown in Figure 10.1.

FIGURE 10.1
Click Yes to save the message in the Drafts folder for later completion.

2. Click **Yes**. Outlook places the current message into the Drafts Folder.

To open the message and continue working on it at another time, follow these steps:

1. Click the **Drafts** folder icon in the My Shortcuts group on the Outlook bar, or choose **Drafts** from the Folder List.

2. Double-click the message to open it. At the top of the Message tab, you'll see a reminder that reads: This Message Has Not Been Sent.

3. Continue your work on the message. If you need to store it again before you're finished, click the **Close** button and answer **Yes** to the message box that asks you to save the file. Alternatively, you can choose to save changes that you have made to the message by clicking the **Save** button on the message toolbar and then closing the message. The message remains in the Drafts folder until you move or send it.

4. When you've actually completed the entire message and are ready to send it, click the **Send** button to send the message.

TIP

> **Create an Outlook Bar Icon for Drafts**   If you would like to place a Drafts folder icon on the Outlook bar when you are in the Outlook Shortcuts group, open the Folder List, pin the Folder List down (click on the push pin that appears when you open the Folders list), and then right-click the **Drafts** folder. On the shortcut menu that appears, select **Add to Outlook Bar**. An icon appears on the Outlook bar for the Drafts folder.

VIEWING SENT ITEMS AND CHANGING DEFAULTS

By default, Outlook saves a copy of all e-mail messages that you send. It keeps these copies in the Sent Items folder, which can be opened using the Sent Items icon found in the My Shortcuts group on the Outlook bar. You can view a list of sent items at any time, and you can open any message in that list to review its contents.

VIEWING SENT ITEMS

To view sent items, follow these steps:

1. In the Outlook bar, choose the **My Shortcuts** group.

 TIP

> **Save Time Using the Folder List**   You can select the Sent Items folder from the Folder List instead of using the icon in the My Shortcuts group.

2. On the Outlook bar, click the **Sent Items** icon; Outlook displays a list of the contents of that folder. Figure 10.2 shows the Sent Items list. All messages you send remain in the Sent Items folder until you delete or move them.

3. (Optional) To view a sent item, select it to view its contents in the Preview pane, or double-click it to open it. When you have finished viewing its contents, click the **Close (x)** button.

 TIP

> **Open the Preview Pane**   If you don't see the Preview pane when you are working in the Sent Items folder, select the **View** menu, and then select **Preview Pane**.

CHANGING SENT E-MAIL DEFAULTS

You can control whether Outlook saves copies of your sent messages (this is also true for unsent messages that are, by default, saved to the Drafts folder). Follow these steps:

1. Select **Tools, Options**, and the Options dialog box appears.

2. Select the **Preferences** tab on the Options dialog box.

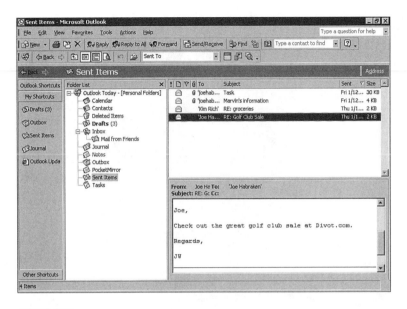

FIGURE 10.2
You can open any sent message by double-clicking it.

3. Click the **E-mail Options** button. The E-mail Options dialog box appears (see Figure 10.3). This dialog box provides a series of check boxes that you can use to toggle several e-mail–related features on and off; to make sure that saved copies of messages are placed in the Sent Items folder, click the **Save Copies of Messages in Sent Items Folder** check box. To have e-mail that is not sent automatically saved in the Outbox, click the **Automatically Save Unsent Messages** check box.

The E-mail Options tab also gives you control over several other features related to the management of your e-mail. More mail option settings are discussed in the next lesson.

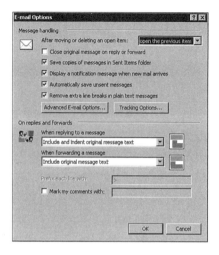

FIGURE 10.3
The E-mail Options dialog box gives you control over various features related to sending and saving unsent e-mail messages.

USING THE ORGANIZE TOOL

You have already learned how to create folders and move e-mail messages to folders to help keep your Outlook information organized (look back at Lesson 9, "Attaching Files and Items to a Message," for more info). Outlook also provides an easy-to-use tool, called the Organize tool, that can help you move, delete, or color code received and sent mail. The Organize tool can even help you deal with annoying junk e-mail that you receive. The Organize feature is able to read the e-mail address of the sender of a particular message and use it to find all the messages in the Inbox that this person has sent. The Organize feature can also use other criteria, such as keywords, to help organize e-mail that you receive. It can actually be configured to delete certain junk mail as soon as you receive it.

The Organize tool provides the Move Message and Create a Rule commands for getting messages out of a particular folder, such as the

Inbox, and placing these items into a different folder. Each of these avenues for moving messages to a particular Outlook folder has its own set of commands in the Organize pane.

MOVING MESSAGES WITH THE ORGANIZER

Suppose that you decide to move a message or messages from a particular person to a new location in Outlook. You can use the Move Message command and place the items into a different folder. However, if you receive additional messages from this individual at a later time, you would have to again manually move the messages to the new location. Wouldn't it be easier to have Outlook move these messages automatically?

To automatically manage future messages from an individual, you can use the Create a Rule command. This creates a rule that moves new messages from an individual to the new location automatically. That way, you can find all the messages from a particular person in the same place when you need them.

PLAIN ENGLISH

Rules   Rules are a set of conditions (such as a particular e-mail address or message content) that you identify to move, delete, or manage incoming e-mail messages.

PLAIN ENGLISH

Rules and Attachments   The rules you create to organize your messages can look at the sender, receiver, message subject, and message text. Attachments to a message are not governed by the rules that you create, so the content of file attachments to a message do not govern how they are handled by the Organize tool or rules.

To use the Organize tool to manage messages from a particular sender, follow these steps:

1. In your Inbox, select a message that you want to work with.

2. Click the **Tools** menu and then click **Organize**, or click the **Organize** button on the toolbar. The Organize window appears (see Figure 10.4).

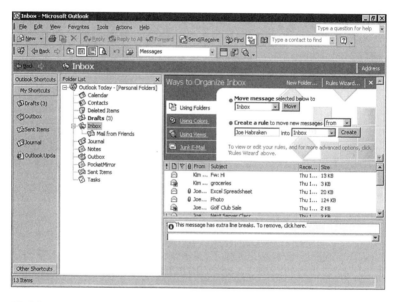

FIGURE 10.4
The Organize tool helps you manage messages using folders, colors, and views.

The Organize tool helps you manage and organize your messages using these methods:

- **Using Folders**—This method is used to move or delete messages; they can be moved to a folder that you create or moved to the Deleted Items folder.

- **Using Colors**—This option enables you to color code messages according to the rule you create.

- **Using Views**—This option uses the rule to categorize messages by their view (Flagged, By Sender, and so on).

- **Junk E-mail**—An option is also provided that helps you deal with junk e-mail.

To manually move the currently selected message in your Inbox, follow these steps:

1. Click **Using Folders**. The e-mail address of the person who sent you the selected e-mail appears in the From box.

2. In the Move Message Selected Below To box, click the drop-down arrow and select the Outlook folder to which you would like to move the message.

3. Click the **Move** button, and the message is moved to the new location.

4. If you want to move other messages, select the message in the Message list and repeat steps 2 and 3.

As already mentioned, you can manage any new messages you receive from a particular individual by creating a rule that automatically moves these new messages to a folder of your choice. To create a new rule for the sender of the currently selected message in your Inbox, follow these steps:

1. Click **Using Folders**. The e-mail address of the person who sent you the selected e-mail appears in the From box.

2. In the Create a Rule to Move New Messages drop-down box, make sure **From** is selected.

3. In the **Into** box, click the drop-down arrow and select the name of the folder to which you want to move the messages.

If you want to move the messages to a folder that is not listed on the drop-down list, click **Other Folder**. The Select Folder list dialog box appears. Double-click the folder that you want to use.

4. When you have selected the folder that the messages are placed in by the rule, click **Create**.

A message box appears in the Organize window (see Figure 10.5).

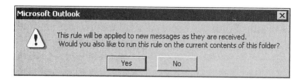

FIGURE 10.5
The new rule can act on existing messages or just new messages.

To run the rule on messages already in the folder (they will be moved by the rule), click **Yes**. If you want the rule to act only on new messages received, click **No**.

That's all there is to creating the new rule. Now, whenever you receive a message from that particular person, the message will be moved to the new location as soon as you receive the message.

USING ORGANIZER TO MANAGE JUNK E-MAIL

When you browse the World Wide Web, you will often come across Web sites that ask you to register with the site using your e-mail address. This is very common with Web sites that provide special content or allow you to enter various contests. After you provide a site with your e-mail address, chances are that they will sell your e-mail address to other Web sites and companies (it's not unlike having your home address placed on a mailing list). This means that it doesn't take very long before you begin to receive junk e-mail messages in Outlook.

The Organize tool also provides you with an automatic strategy for dealing with annoying junk mail. Click **Junk E-mail** in the Organize window (see Figure 10.6). The Organize tool enables you to either color code junk mail and adult-content e-mail or move these kinds of e-mail to a folder of your choice. In most situations, junk e-mail and other unwanted e-mail can be moved directly to the Deleted Items folder, and the items can then be easily discarded. Outlook automatically identifies these types of mail messages as you receive them by using a list of keywords as identifiers.

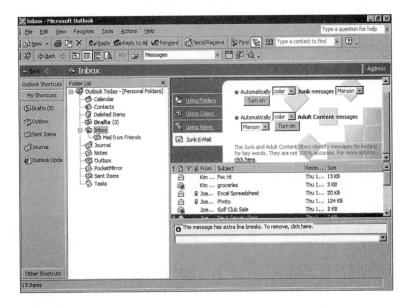

FIGURE 10.6
The Organize tool's Junk E-mail manager can help you deal with incoming junk mail.

To color code junk messages or adult-content messages, make sure the Automatically drop-down box for each junk-mail type (junk messages or adult content) contains the choice **Color**. Then, use the appropriate color drop-down box to select the color you want to use to code these messages as they are received. After you have selected the color, click the **Turn On** button to begin color coding all new messages that are identified as junk mail or adult-content mail by Outlook.

To send junk messages or adult-content messages directly to a specific folder (such as Deleted Items), select **Move** in the Automatically drop-down box for either type of message. In the Messages To drop-down box for either message type, select **Junk Mail** or **Deleted Items** to send mail messages directly to either of these folders. You can also send these messages directly to an alternative folder of your choice by clicking **Other Folder**. After you have selected the folder you want to send these messages to, click the **Turn On** button. Messages that Outlook identifies as junk mail or adult content are sent directly to the folder you specified.

You can also click the **For More Options Click Here** selection at the bottom of the Organize pane to access additional options related to junk mail and adult content. Links are provided so that you can access the list of e-mail addresses that you have identified as sources of junk mail or adult content. Any e-mail address on these lists is used to identify incoming e-mail that should be color coded or moved to a specific folder by the Organize tool. After you have completed your selections in the Organize window, click its **Close** button.

You can quickly add e-mail addresses to the Junk E-mail or Adult Content list by right-clicking any message in your Inbox. A shortcut menu appears; point at Junk E-mail on the menu, and then select either **Add to Junk Senders List** or **Add to Adult Content Senders List** from the cascading menu that opens. This adds this e-mail to the list, marking it as a source of junk mail or adult-content messages.

CREATING ADVANCED RULES WITH THE WIZARD

If the Organize tool isn't able to manage your e-mail to the degree you desire, you can create more advanced rules for managing messages using the Outlook Rules Wizard. The Rules Wizard enables you to create pretty sophisticated rules using simple sentences.

To open the Rules Wizard, follow these steps:

1. Click **Tools, Rules Wizard**. The Rules Wizard dialog box appears (see Figure 10.7).

   All the rules previously created using the Organize tool appear in the Rules Description box. You can copy, modify, rename, or delete a rule in this dialog box. You can also change a rule's priority by selecting a rule and then moving it up or down using the Move Up or Move Down buttons.

FIGURE 10.7
The Rules Wizard helps you create rules for managing mail messages.

2. To create a new rule, click the **New** button. The Rules Wizard walks you through the rule-creation process. The first screen asks you to choose either to create the rule from an existing template or create a new, blank rule. Step 3 describes creating a rule from scratch (although both possibilities offer similar options from the wizard).

3. Click the **Start from a Blank Rule** option button. Now you can select the type of rule you want to create, such as **Check**

Messages When They Arrive (see Figure 10.8), and then click **Next**.

FIGURE 10.8
In the Rules Wizard, you select the type of rule you want to create.

4. Select the type of rule you want to create, and then click **Next**.

5. The next screen asks you to select conditions that are to be used by the new rule (see Figure 10.9). These conditions range from messages sent directly to you, to e-mail addresses that you have placed on your junk e-mail list. Use the check boxes provided to select the condition or conditions for your new rule. Click Next to continue.

TIP

> **Conditions That Require Input from You** Some conditions such as From People or Distribution List or Specific Words require that you provide a list of people for the condition to use or certain words. Conditions requiring additional information have an underlined selection for you to click.

FIGURE 10.9
You select the conditions that are to be used by the rule.

6. The next screen asks you to decide what the rule should do to a message that meets the rules criteria. Several choices are provided, such as Move It to the Specified Folder or Delete It (see Figure 10.10). Make your selections in the check boxes provided. Click **Next** to continue.

7. The next screen provides you with the opportunity to add any exceptions to the rule. These exceptions can include Except If Sent Only to Me or Except Where My Name Is in the To Box. You add the exceptions by clicking the check box next to a particular exception. You can select multiple exceptions or choose to have no exceptions to the rules. Then, click **Next** to continue.

8. The Rules Wizard's final screen asks you to type a name for your new rule. After you've done that, click **Finish**. The new rule appears in the Rules Wizard dialog box. You can create more new rules or click **OK** to close the dialog box.

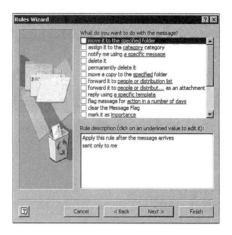

FIGURE 10.10
You determine the type of action you want Outlook to take when it finds a message that meets the rule's criteria.

 TIP

> **Delete "Bad" Rules**   If you find that a rule or rules that
> you have created are actually doing things to messages
> that you hadn't planned, you can delete the rules. Rules
> created with the Organize tool can also be deleted in
> this manner. Open the Rules Wizard (click **Tools**, then
> **Rules Wizard**). In the Rules Wizard dialog box, select
> rules that you want to delete and then select **Delete**.
> They will be removed from the rule list.

When you use the Rules Wizard for the first time, you may want to
create a simple rule or two that handle messages that you do not con-
sider extremely important. A poorly designed rule could delete important messages that you receive. A good general rule is to use the
Organize tool first and let it create simple rules, and if you need more
advanced message-management help, use the Rules Wizard.

In this lesson, you learned to save a draft and view sent items. You also learned how to use the Organize tool and the Rules Wizard to manage Outlook messages. In the next lesson, you will learn to set various Outlook e-mail options and work with message flags.

LESSON 11
Setting Mail Options

In this lesson, you learn how to set options for messages related to message priority and the delivery of messages. You also learn how to work with message flags.

WORKING WITH MESSAGE OPTIONS

Outlook provides options that enable you to mark any message with certain options that emphasize a certain aspect of the message's importance. You can use Priority status so that the recipient knows you need a quick response. Using a sensitivity rating makes it so that not just anyone can change your message after it is sent. With other options you can enable the recipients of your message to vote on an issue by including voting buttons in your message and having the replies sent to a specific location.

You also can set delivery options. For example, you can schedule the delivery of a message for a specified delivery time or date if you don't want to send it right now.

CAUTION

Recognizing Priority Flags   Not all e-mail packages recognize the priority flags that you place on messages you send. These priority flags work ideally in a network situation, where Outlook is the e-mail client for all users. Microsoft's Outlook Express e-mail client also has the capability to recognize priority flags that you use on sent messages.

To set message options, open a new e-mail and click the **Options** button on the toolbar (or select **View, Options**). As you can see in Figure
11.1, the Message Options dialog box is separated into four areas. The
next four sections discuss each group of options in detail.

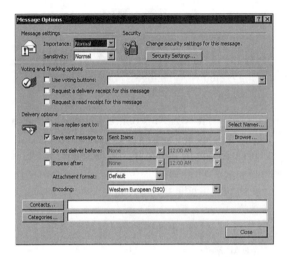

FIGURE 11.1
Use the Message Options dialog box to govern how your message is sent.

MESSAGE SETTINGS

In the Message Settings area, set any of the following options for your
message:

- Click the **Importance** drop-down arrow and choose a priority
  level of **Low, Normal**, or **High** from the list. (Alternatively,
  you could click the **Importance High** or **Importance Low**
  button on the message's toolbar when you compose the message.) When importance isn't specified, the message is given
  Normal importance.

- Click the **Sensitivity** drop-down arrow and choose one of the following options:
  - **Normal**—Use this option to indicate that the message contents are standard or customary.
  - **Personal**—Use this option to suggest that the message contents are of a personal nature.
  - **Private**—Use this option to prevent the message from being edited (text changes, copy, paste, and so on) after you send it.
  - **Confidential**—Use this option to indicate that the message contents are restricted or private. Confidential messages can be edited by the recipient. Marking the message Confidential is only to suggest how the recipient should handle the contents of the message.

TIP

> **Mark All Messages As Private**   You can mark all your new messages as private automatically. Choose **Tools**, **Options**. On the **Preferences** tab, click the **E-Mail Options** button. In the E-Mail Options dialog box, click the **Advanced E-Mail Options** button. Use the **Sensitivity** drop-down box at the bottom of the Advanced E-Mail Options dialog box to set the default sensitivity for all your new e-mail messages.

Outlook also supplies you with options related to the security settings for a message. You can choose to encrypt the contents of your message or add a digital signature to the message.

To set the security option for the message, click the **Security Settings** button. This opens the Security Properties dialog box, as shown in Figure 11.2.

If you want to encrypt the message, click the **Encrypt Message Contents and Attachments** check box. If you want, you can also add a digital signature to the message that verifies you are the sender; click the **Add Digital Signature to This Message** check box.

FIGURE 11.2
You can set security options for a message, such as encryption and the use of a digital signature.

KEEPING TRACK

Encryption   Messages are coded so that they remain secure until the recipient opens them.

KEEPING TRACK

Digital Signature   A digital ID that is electronically stamped on messages that you send. This allows recipients of the message to verify that the message is truly sent by you.

Before you can use either the encryption or the digital-signature features, you must obtain a digital ID, which is also often called a certificate. Digital IDs are issued by an independent certifying authority.

Microsoft's certifying authority of choice is VeriSign Digital ID. For a fee, you can obtain, download, and install your digital ID from VeriSign by following the steps on their Web page at `http://digitalid.verisign.com/`.

Most e-mail traffic doesn't really require encryption or the use of digital signatures. You will have to determine for yourself whether your e-mails require extra security precautions such as encryption and digital signatures.

VOTING AND TRACKING OPTIONS

The Voting and Tracking Options enable you to control special features such as voting buttons (these allow recipients of the message to reply with a click of the mouse), which supply you with the means to track the receipt of your message. The delivery and read notification options allow you to receive notification that the recipient of the message has received the message or opened and read it, respectively.

- Select the **Use Voting Buttons** check box to add the default choices (Approve and Reject) to your message. You can also add Yes and No choices or Yes, No, and Maybe choices using the drop-down list to the right of the Use Voting Buttons check box. If you want to provide other choices, enter your own text into the text box (using semicolons to break up your choices). When you send a message with voting buttons to several people, you can view a summary of all the voting results by clicking the voting summary message on any of the e-mail responses.

- Select **Request a Delivery Receipt for This Message** to receive an e-mail notification that the intended recipient has received the message.

- Select **Request a Read Receipt for This Message** to receive e-mail confirmation that the recipient has opened the message.

DELIVERY OPTIONS

In addition to voting and tracking options, you can set certain delivery options, such as having replies sent to individuals you select. You can also choose a folder where a copy of the message is saved, or schedule the time of the delivery. In the Delivery Options area of the Message Options dialog box, choose any of the following check boxes:

- Normally, a reply to an e-mail message returns to the e-mail address of the sender. Sometimes, especially if you have multiple e-mail accounts, you might want replies to your message to go to a different e-mail address than the one you're sending from. Choose the **Have Replies Sent To** check box and specify in the text box the e-mail address to which you want the replies sent (see Figure 11.3). You can use the **Select Names** button to view your Contacts or Outlook Address Book and choose an e-mail address or addresses from the selected list.

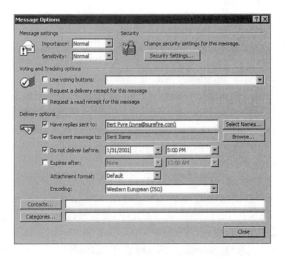

FIGURE 11.3
You can specify that responses to a message be sent to specific e-mail addresses (including or excluding your own).

- Select the **Save Sent Message To** check box to save your message to a folder other than the Sent Items folder. The Sent Items folder is specified by default, but you can choose to save the sent message to any folder in Outlook. Use the **Browse** button and the resulting Select Folder dialog box to specify a particular folder.

- Select the **Do Not Deliver Before** option to specify a delivery date. Click the down arrow in the text box beside the option to display a calendar on which you can select the day. This option enables you to send out e-mail even when you are not at your computer (or in the office). The message will be held in your Outbox folder until the specified time. If you are using Internet e-mail, your computer and Outlook must be up and running for the e-mail to be sent. In a corporate environment where Exchange Server is used, the e-mail is stored on the mail server and is sent automatically on the delivery date.

- Select the **Expires After** check box to include a day, date, and time of expiration. You can click the down arrow in the text box to display a calendar from which you can choose a date, or you can enter the date and time yourself. Messages marked to expire are made unavailable after the expiration date. This means the message is basically recalled from any computer where the message has not been read (this feature works only in networked environments using Microsoft Exchange Server).

The delivery options are really great in cases where someone other than you needs to keep track of the responses related to an e-mail message that you sent or in cases where you don't want to immediately deliver a message using the Do Not Deliver Before option. Using the Expire option means that people who have been on vacation won't have to read old messages that you have sent; they will no longer be available because of the expiration date.

ASSIGNING CONTACTS AND CATEGORIES TO A MESSAGE

The Message Options dialog box also enables you to link a contact or contacts to a message. Linking a contact (or contacts) to a message allows you to view the message on that contact's Activities tab (when you are viewing the contact's actual record in the Contacts folder). The use of the Activities tab on a contact's record is discussed in Lesson 13, "Creating a Contacts List."

CAUTION

Do Contact Links and Categories Appear on Sent Messages? When you link contacts and categories to messages, you are actually just applying organizational tags to the e-mails. You can then view all the e-mail sent to a particular contact in the Contacts folder or sort sent e-mail by a particular category. The recipient of e-mail that you have tagged in this manner does not know that you created the link.

To assign a contact link to the message, click the **Contacts** button in the Message Options dialog box. The Select Contacts dialog box opens, showing all your contacts. Double-click a contact to add it to the Contacts box on the Message Options dialog box. Now the sent message is linked to a particular contact or contacts and can be accessed for later consideration when you are working with that contact or contacts in the Contacts folder.

Another option that Outlook provides for organizing sent messages is the use of categories. You can assign your messages to different categories, such as Business, Goals, Hot Contacts, Phone Calls, and so on. You set the category for a message in the Categories dialog box.

> **PLAIN ENGLISH**
>
> **Categories**   Categories offer a way of organizing mes-
> sages to make them easier to find, sort, print, and man-
> age. To find all the items in one category, choose **Tools**,
> **Find Items**. Click the **More Choices** tab, choose
> **Categories**, and check the category for which you're
> searching.

To assign a category, follow these steps:

1. In the Message Options dialog box, click the **Categories** button. The Categories dialog box appears (see Figure 11.4).

FIGURE 11.4
Organize your messages with categories.

2. To assign an existing category, select the category or categories that best suit your message from the Available
   Categories list. To assign a new category, enter a new category into the **Item(s) Belong to These Categories** text box,
   and then click the **Add to List** button.

3. Click **OK** to close the Categories dialog box and return to the
   Message Options dialog box.

TIP

> **Create Your Own Categories**   If you want to create a new
> category to assign to your e-mail messages, click the
> **Master Category List** button on the Categories dialog box.
> The Master Category List dialog box appears. Type the
> name of the new category in the New category box, and
> then click **Add** (repeat as necessary). To return to the
> Categories dialog box, click **OK**. Your new categories
> appear in the Categories dialog box.

When you have set all the options for the current message, click the
Close button to close the Message Options box and return to the message window.

The whole point of tagging sent messages with categories is so that
you can view messages by category when you open the Sent Items
folder. For example, you might want to quickly check the messages
that have been tagged with the Competition category. Changing the
view of a particular folder, such as the Sent Items folder, is handled
using the View menu.

1. Use the Folder List to open the Sent Items folder.

2. To view the messages by category, select the **View** menu,
   point at **Current View**, and then select **Customize Current
   View**. The View Summary dialog box opens.

3. Click the **Group By** button on the View Summary dialog
   box. The Group By dialog box opens as shown in Figure
   11.5.

4. Click the **Group Items By** drop-down list and select
   Categories, and then click **OK** to close the dialog box.

5. Click **OK** to close the View Summary dialog box.

6. When you return to the Sent Items folder, a list of the categories that you have assigned to your sent messages appear.

To view the messages listed under a particular category, click the **plus** (+) symbol to the left of a particular category.

FIGURE 11.5
View your messages by category.

CAUTION

Now My View Is All Messed Up!   To remove the custom view, repeat steps 2–5; in step 4 select **None** in the Group By drop-down box. This returns your view of the folder to the default view.

USING MESSAGE FLAGS

Another tool for tagging messages is a message flag. A message flag enables you to mark a message as important, either as a reminder for yourself or as a signal to the message's recipient. When you send a message flag, a red flag icon appears in the recipient's message list, and Outlook adds text at the top of the message telling which type of flag you are sending. In addition, you can add a due date to the flag, and that date appears at the top of the message.

The following list outlines the types of flags you can send in Outlook:

Call   No Response Necessary

Do Not Forward   Read

Follow Up	Reply
For Your Information	Reply to All
Forward	Review

Using these various flags is like sticking a brief note on the message that provides you with a clue as to what type of follow-up might be required by a particular message. To use a message flag, follow these steps:

1. Open a new message or existing message that you want to flag. In the message window, click **Actions** and then select **Follow Up**. The Flag for Follow Up dialog box appears (see Figure 11.6).

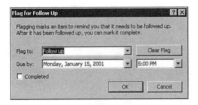

FIGURE 11.6
Flag a message to show its importance or as a reminder for your follow-up.

2. Click the **Flag To** drop-down arrow, and choose the flag type you want to add to the message.

3. Click the **Due By** drop-down arrow and use the calendar that appears to enter a date into the text box. Use the **Time** drop-down box to set a specific time. Assigning a due date and time makes you act on the message as dictated by the flag by a particular date.

4. Click **OK** to return to the message window.

Figure 11.7 shows the Inbox with some flagged messages.

Marking messages with the Follow Up flag is a great way to remind yourself that you need to attend to a particular issue. Flagging messages for your e-mail recipients helps them prioritize responses, so you receive the needed reply within a particular time frame.

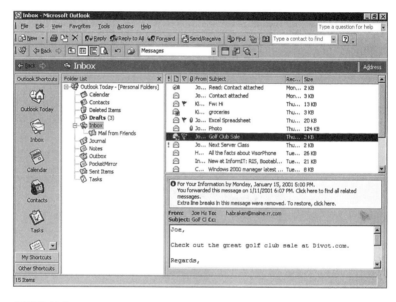

FIGURE 11.7
Flagged messages "pop out" of a particular folder, reminding you to deal with them.

When you double-click a flagged message and open it in a message window (see Figure 11.8), the flag type appears at the top of the message, just above the From box.

Viewing the flag type on the message provides you with a quick reminder as to what your next action should be regarding the particular message.

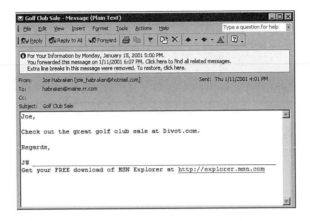

FIGURE 11.8
To view the type of flag attached, open the message.

In this lesson, you learned to set options for messages including options related to the delivery and tracking of messages. You also learned how to flag messages. In the next lesson, you will learn to use the Contact and Outlook address books.

LESSON 12

Using the Outlook Address Books

In this lesson, you learn about different Outlook address books and how to import lists to Outlook from other applications.

UNDERSTANDING THE OUTLOOK ADDRESS BOOKS

Outlook has the capability to access different stores or lists of information that can provide you with people's e-mail addresses and other contact information, such as phone numbers and addresses. The address books that you can access include the Personal Address Book, your Contacts list, and other directory lists that are provided by other e-mail systems and communication servers. For example, in a corporate network, a Microsoft Exchange Server can provide you with a Global Address list that is shared by all users on the Exchange network. The e-mail address of any users on the network are then easily found in one resource.

> ### KEEPING TRACK
> **The Contacts List**   You might notice contacts in the list of address books; this list contains entries you create in your Contacts list. For more information about the Contacts list, see Lesson 13, "Creating a Contacts List."

Where your e-mail addresses and other contact information are stored depends on whether you are using Outlook on a corporate network that uses Active Directory, a network that uses Exchange Server, or as a standalone product where you use an Internet e-mail account.

However, no matter where your contact information is kept, Outlook makes it easy for you to access your different address books using the Address Book feature.

USING THE ADDRESS BOOK

The Address Book is basically a launch pad that allows you to access information lists (they are all considered address books) that contain e-mail addresses and other contact information. Because you create your own Contacts list, you always have this resource available, even if you aren't connected to a special network server and you access your e-mail by connecting to the Internet. You can find more information about building your Contacts list in Lesson 13. Outlook also has the capability to access Web-based address directories such as Bigfoot and InfoSpace, which are both Web directories that can help you find people's e-mail addresses.

You can open the Address Book feature by clicking the **To** button or **Cc** button on a new message or by clicking the **Address Book** icon on the Outlook toolbar. After the Address Book dialog box is open, as shown in Figure 12.1, you can use the **Show Names from the** drop-down list to select the specific address book (such as your Personal Address Book or Contacts list) that you want to view.

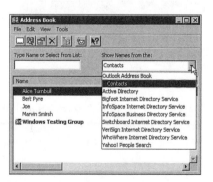

FIGURE 12.1
The Address Book enables you to access any of your address books.

Finding Records in an Address Book

The Address Book dialog box also makes it easy for you to search through a particular address book for a particular person. In the Type Name box, begin to type the name of a contact you want to find in the list; as soon as you type enough of the contact's name for Outlook to find that particular contact, it will be highlighted in the list provided.

In cases where you want to search for a record or records by a particular character string (such as all records in the address book that have the last name of Smith), the Address Book provides you with a Find dialog box.

 Click the **Find Items** button on the Address Book toolbar. The Find dialog box appears as shown in Figure 12.2.

FIGURE 12.2
You can search a particular address book by keywords or text strings using the Find dialog box.

Type your search string into the Find Names Containing box. Then, click **OK** to run the search. The search results appear in the Address Book dialog box. Only the records that match your search parameters appear in the list.

ADDING RECORDS TO AN ADDRESS BOOK

You can also add records to any of the address books that you have access to. For example, you can add records to your Personal Address book or to your Contacts list directly in the Address Book window. Keep in mind that in a corporate environment, your network adminis-trator likely controls some address books, such as the Global Address Book. This means that you won't be able to add information to these address books; you can use them only as resources to find information such as e-mail addresses.

To add a record to an address book that you do control:

1. In the Address Book dialog box, make sure that you have the address book selected that you want to add the new record to.

2. Click the **New Entry** button on the Address Book toolbar. The New Entry dialog box appears (see Figure 12.3).

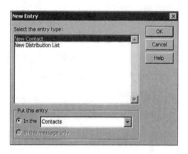

FIGURE 12.3
You can add new records to address books using the New Entry dialog box.

3. Use the **Put This Entry in the** drop-down box at the bottom of the New Entry dialog box to make sure that your new record ends up in the correct address book. To add a new record (a new contact, for example), click **New Contact** and then click **OK**.

PLAIN ENGLISH

Distribution List   A distribution list allows you to create a record that includes the e-mail addresses for several people. This makes it easy to send e-mails to a group of people. You can create distribution lists in the New Entry dialog box. You will learn how to create distribution lists in the next lesson.

4. A blank record appears for your new entry. Enter the appropriate information for the new record, such as the person's name, e-mail address, and so on into the appropriate text boxes. When you have finished entering the information, click **OK** to save the new entry. In the case of new contacts added to the Contacts list, click the **Save and Close** button.

The blank records that open for your new entries will look slightly different, depending on the address book in which you are creating the new record. In the case of new contacts (which is discussed in the next lesson), you can enter information for the new entry that includes the person's address, phone number, fax number, and even a Web page address. Some address books may allow you to enter only the name and e-mail address of the person.

TIP

🖾 **Create a New Message from the Address Book Dialog Box**   If you opened the Address Book using the **Address Book** icon on the Outlook toolbar (or selected **Tools, Address Book**), you can open a new message for any of the contacts listed in one of the address books. Select the particular person, and then click the **New Message** icon on the Address Book icon. A new message opens addressed to that particular person.

IMPORTING ADDRESS BOOKS AND CONTACT LISTS

If you are migrating from another personal information manager or e-mail client and want to import your address book or Contacts list, Outlook contains different conversion filters for this purpose. Outlook even provides you with an Import/Export Wizard that walks you through the steps of importing address lists and address books from these other software packages.

To start the Outlook Import/Export Wizard, follow these steps:

1. Click **File**, and then select **Import and Export**. The Outlook Import and Export Wizard opens (see Figure 12.4).

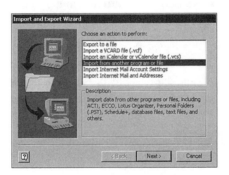

FIGURE 12.4
The Import and Export Wizard walks you through the process of importing your old address books or information from other applications.

2. On the first wizard screen, you can choose to import e-mail and contacts information from another e-mail client, such as Outlook Express or Netscape, by selecting **Import Internet Mail and Addresses**. Then, click **Next**.

3. On the next screen, select the e-mail client, such as Outlook Express, that holds the information that you will import to

Outlook (remember that this feature imports e-mail messages and address information from the e-mail client to Outlook). Then, click **Next**.

4. The next wizard screen asks you to select the Outlook address book that will hold the imported information. Select the **Personal Address Book** option button or the **Outlook Contacts Folder** option button to specify the destination for the imported records. Additional option buttons on this screen allow you to specify how duplicate records are handled; select one of the following:

- Replace duplicates with items imported; this option replaces any records currently in the address book with duplicates from the imported file.

- Allow duplicates to be created; any duplicates currently in the address book are not overwritten during the import, and duplicate records are placed in the address book.

- Do not import duplicate items; any duplicate items found in the address book that is being imported are not imported into Outlook.

5. After making your selections, click **Finish**.

The e-mail messages and the e-mail address records are imported into the Outlook address book that you chose. A message appears letting you know how many records were imported. The address records are placed in the address book that you chose. Imported e-mail is placed in the appropriate Outlook folder, such as your Inbox and Sent Items folders.

TIP

> **Importing Information from Database Programs**   If you
> want to import address records or other information from
> programs such as Microsoft Access or Lotus Notes,
> select the Import from another program or file option on
> the initial Import and Export Wizard screen. You are
> then walked through the steps of selecting the program
> and file that holds the data that you want to import. You
> will have the option of selecting the Outlook Contacts
> list or another address book, such as the Personal
> Address Book, to hold the information after it is
> imported.

EXPORTING OUTLOOK ADDRESS RECORDS

There might be occasions where you would like to take the records in
one of your Outlook address books, such as the Contacts list, and
export this information to another software package. For example, you
may want to place all the records in your Contacts list in an Access
database file (this is particularly useful in cases where you might be
using Outlook to hold information about your customers or clients).
Outlook records can be exported using the Import and Export Wizard.

Follow these steps:

1. Click **File**, and then select **Import and Export**. The Outlook
   Import and Export Wizard opens.

2. Select **Export to a File**, and then click **Next**.

3. On the next screen, you are provided with a list of file types
   that you can use for your export file (see Figure 12.5). Select
   a file type, such as Microsoft Access, and then click **Next**.

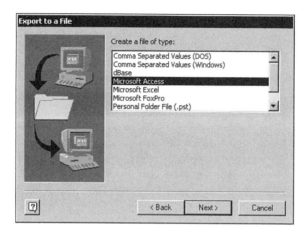

FIGURE 12.5
The Import and Export Wizard walks you through the process of importing your old address books or information from other applications.

4. On the next screen, you are asked to select the Outlook folder that contains the information that you will export. Select the appropriate folder such as **Contacts**. Then, click **Next**.

5. On the next screen, type a name for the file in the Save Exported File As: box. If you want to specify a specific location on your computer for the file to be saved, use the **Browse** button to open the Browse dialog box. When you have returned to the wizard (click **OK** to close the Browse dialog box), click **Next**.

6. The next screen lists the folder that will be exported. Click **Finish**. The export file is created.

After the information has been exported to the new file (it is actually copied to the new file; your Contacts list remains intact in Outlook), you can open the file using the destination application. For example, if you created an Access database using the export feature, you can open the file created using Microsoft Access.

In this lesson, you learned to use the Address Book feature to find records and to create new entries in your various address books. You also learned how to import address books from other software programs. In the next lesson, you will learn to work with the Outlook Contacts feature.

LESSON 13
Creating a Contacts List

In this lesson, you learn how to create and view a Contacts list and how to send mail to someone on your Contacts list. You also learn how to create a distribution list.

CREATING A NEW CONTACT

You use the Contacts folder to create, store, and access your Contacts list. You can enter any or all of the following information about each contact:

- Name
- Job title
- Company name
- Address (street, city, state, ZIP code, and country)
- Phone (business, home, business fax, mobile)
- E-mail address
- Web page address
- Comments, notes, or descriptions
- Categories

You also can edit the information at any time, add new contacts, or delete contacts from the list. To open the Contacts folder and create a new contact, follow these steps:

1. To open the Contacts folder, click the **Contacts** shortcut on the Outlook bar. The Contacts folder opens.

2. To create a new contact, select **Actions** and then choose **New Contact**, or click the **New Contact** button on the Standard toolbar. The Contact dialog box appears, with the General tab displayed (see Figure 13.1).

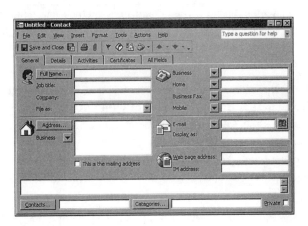

FIGURE 13.1
You can enter as much or as little information about each contact as you need.

3. Enter the contact's name into the Full Name text box. If you want to add more detailed information for the name, click the **Full Name** button to display the Check Full Name dialog box, and then enter the contact's title and full name (including first, middle, and last names) and any suffix you want to include. Click **OK** to close the Check Full Name dialog box and return to the Contact dialog box.

4. Press the **Tab** key to navigate from one field in this dialog box to the next. After the name field, the insert point moves down to the contact's job title and then the company name. This information is optional.

5. In the **File As** drop-down box, enter or select the method by which you want to file your contact's names. You can choose **Last Name First** or **First Name First**, or you can enter your own filing system, such as by company or state.

 TIP

> **Keep It Simple**   The default filing method for contacts is last name first, which makes it easy to quickly find the contact when you need it.

6. Enter the address into the Address box and choose whether the address is **Business**, **Home**, or **Other**. Alternatively, you can click the **Address** button to enter the street, city, state, ZIP code, and country in specified areas instead of all within the text block. You can add a second address (the Home address, for example) if you want. Address information is optional.

7. In the **Phone** drop-down lists, choose the type of phone number—Business, Callback, Car, Home Fax, ISDN, Pager, and so on—and then enter the number. You can enter up to 19 numbers into each of the four drop-down boxes in the Phone area of the dialog box.

8. You can enter up to three e-mail addresses into the **E-Mail** text box. The box below the e-mail address allows you to enter how the e-mail address appears when you send a message to a person (for example, smith@mail.com could appear as Bob Smith); in the **Web Page Address** text box, enter the address for the company or contact's URL on the World Wide Web.

If you have more than one e-mail address for a contact, the first number or address in the list serves as the default. For example, when e-mailing a contact, the first e-mail address in the list is placed in the To box on the new message. If you want to use a different e-mail address for the contact, double-click the contact's name in the Message To box and select one of the other e-mail addresses in the contact's Properties box. When you want to call a contact for whom you have multiple numbers, a drop-down list appears in the New Call dialog box that enables you to choose the appropriate number.

PLAIN ENGLISH

> **URL (Uniform Resource Locator)**   The address for a Web page on the World Wide Web. A typical URL is written `http://www.companyname.com`, such as `http://www.mcp.com`.

9. In the comment text box, enter any descriptions, comments, or other pertinent information. Then, select or enter a category to classify the contact.

10. After you have finished entering the new contact information, click the **Save and Close** button to return to the Contacts folder. You can also save the new contact by opening the **File** menu and choosing one of the following commands:

- **Save**—Saves the record and closes the Contact dialog box.

- **Save and New**—Saves the record and clears the Contact dialog box so that you can enter a new contact.

PLAIN ENGLISH

Other Tabs in the Contacts Window   Most of the information that you need to enter for a contact is contained on the General tab. You can also add additional information, such as the person's nickname or spouse's name, on the Details tab. The Certificates tab allows you to specify a certificate to use to send encrypted e-mail to this particular contact (Certificates are discussed in Lesson 11, "Setting Mail Options").

You can edit the information for a contact at any time by double-clicking the contact's name in the Contacts list; this displays the contact's information window. Alternatively, you can work on the fields in a record directly in the Contacts list window. Click within the information listed below a contact's name (such as the phone number or address) to position the insertion point in the text and then delete or enter text. Press **Enter** to complete the modifications you've made and move to the next contact in the list.

VIEWING THE CONTACTS LIST

By default, you see the contacts in Address Cards view (Address Cards appear in the Current View list on the Outlook Advanced toolbar). The information you see displays the contact's name and other data, such as addresses and phone numbers. The contact's company name, job title, and comments, however, are not displayed by default. Figure 13.2 shows the Contacts list in the default Address Cards view.

You can use the horizontal scrollbar to view more contacts, or you can click a letter in the index (on the right side of the screen) to display contacts beginning with that letter in the first column of the list.

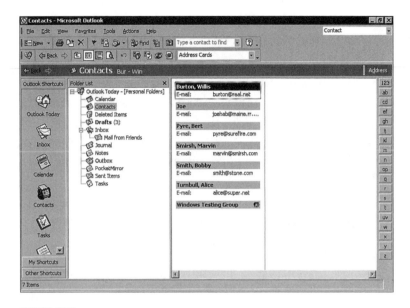

FIGURE 13.2
View your contacts in Address Cards view.

You can change how you view the contacts in the list by choosing one of these options from the Current View drop-down list on the Standard toolbar:

- **Address Cards**—Displays full name, addresses, and phone numbers of the contacts, depending on the amount of information you've entered, in a card format.

- **Detailed Address Cards**—Displays full name, job title, company, addresses, phone numbers, e-mail addresses, categories, and comments in a card format.

- **Phone List**—Displays full name, job title, company, File As name, department, phone numbers, and categories in a table, organizing each entry horizontally in rows and columns.

- **By Category**—Displays contacts in rows by categories. The information displayed is the same as what's displayed in a phone list.

- **By Company**—Displays contacts in rows, grouped by their company. The information displayed is the same as what's displayed in a phone list.

- **By Location**—Displays contacts grouped by country. The information displayed is the same as what's displayed in a phone list.

- **By Follow-Up Flag**—Displays contacts grouped by follow-up flags. The view also displays the due date for the follow-up that you specified when you marked the contact with a flag (flags are discussed in Lesson 10, "Saving Drafts and Organizing Messages," and can be assigned to Contacts the same as they are assigned to e-mail messages).

VIEWING A CONTACTS ACTIVITIES TAB

Although the Contacts folder provides different views for perusing the actual contacts in the Contacts list, these views really don't give you any indication of the messages that you have sent to a particular contact or the tasks that you might have assigned to a particular contact (assigning a task to a contact is covered later in this lesson).

You can view all the activities related to a particular contact on the contact's Activities tab. With the Contacts folder open, follow these steps:

1. Double-click a contact in the Contacts folder to open the contact.

2. Click the **Activities** tab on the contact's window. All the activities, such as sent and received e-mails and any assigned tasks, appear in the Activities pane (see Figure 13.3).

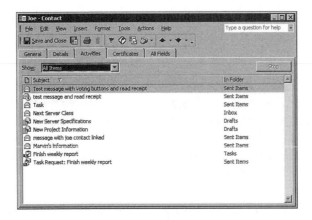

FIGURE 13.3
You can view all the activities related to a particular contact.

3. To see a subset of the Activities list, click the **Show** drop-down box. You can choose to view only E-mail, Notes, or Upcoming Tasks/Appointments related to that particular contact (any items that you delete in the Activities list are removed from the list and the folder that contained them).

4. You open any of the items on the Activities list by double-clicking that item. Close an opened item by clicking its **Close** (**x**) button.

5. When you have finished viewing the activities related to a particular contact, you can close the contact's window.

USING DISTRIBUTION LISTS

If you find that you are sending e-mail messages or assigning tasks to multiple recipients, you might want to create a distribution list. A distribution list enables you to group several contacts. Then, to send an e-mail to all the contacts in the distribution list, you address the e-mail with the name of the distribution list.

The distribution lists that you create are listed in your Contacts folder. You can open an existing distribution list by double-clicking it. You can then add or delete members of the list.

To create a distribution list, follow these steps:

1. Select the **Actions** menu, and then select **New Distribution List**, or you can right-click an empty space of the Contacts folder and select **New Distribution List** from the shortcut menu that appears. The Distribution List window appears (see Figure 13.4).

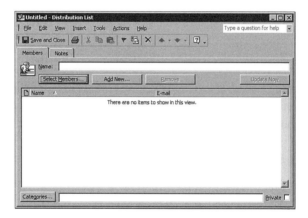

FIGURE 13.4
You can add contacts to a distribution list for mass e-mail mailings.

2. To enter a name for the distribution list, type the name into the Name box.

3. To add contacts to the distribution list, click the **Select Members** button, which opens the Select Members dialog box. Use the **Show Names from the** drop-down list to select the address book, such as the Contacts list, that you want to use to add names to the distribution list.

4. Select a contact to add to the distribution list, and then click the **Members** button to add the contact to the list (see Figure 13.5).

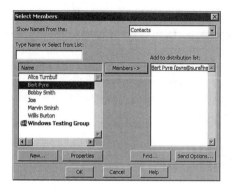

FIGURE 13.5
Add your contacts to the list from any of your address books.

5. To select multiple contacts at once, hold down the **Ctrl** key, click the mouse on each contact, and then click the **Members** button.

6. When you have finished adding the contacts to the distribution list, click the **OK** button on the Select Members dialog box. You are returned to the Distribution List window.

7. To save the distribution list, click the **Save and Close** button on the list's toolbar.

After you have saved the distribution list, it appears as a contact listing in your Contacts folder. You can use the distribution list's name in the To box of an e-mail message to send the message to all the contacts listed in the distribution list.

If you find that you want to remove names from a distribution list, open the distribution list from the Contacts folder. In the Distribution List window, select the name or names you want to remove from the list. Then, click the **Remove** button. Make sure that you save the changes that you have made to the distribution list.

Add People to the Distribution List Who Are Not Current Contacts   If you want to add names and associated e-mail addresses for people who are not in an address book to a distribution list, click the **Add New** button in the Distribution List window. The Add New dialog box allows you to enter a name and e-mail address for a new member of the distribution list.

COMMUNICATING WITH A CONTACT

You can send messages to any of your contacts, arrange meetings, assign tasks, or even send a letter to a contact from within Outlook (this also includes any distribution lists that you have created in the Contacts folder). To communicate with a contact, make sure you're in the Contacts folder. You do not need to open the specific contact's information window to perform any of the following procedures.

SENDING MESSAGES

To send a message to a contact, you must make sure you've entered an e-mail address in the General tab of the Contact dialog box for that particular contact. If Outlook cannot locate the e-mail address, it displays a message dialog box letting you know.

To send a message from the Contacts folder, select the contact, select **Actions**, and then select **New Message to Contact** (or you can right-click the contact or the distribution list and select **New Message to Contact** from the shortcut menu that appears).

 In the Untitled - Message dialog box, enter the subject and message and set any options you want. When you're ready to send the message, click the **Send** button.

SCHEDULING A MEETING WITH A CONTACT

To schedule a meeting with a contact (or with contacts contained in a distribution list), you must first select the contact or distribution list (as with sending mail messages, the contacts involved must have an e-mail address). After you've selected the contact or list, select **Actions**, and then select **New Meeting Request to Contact** to open the Untitled - Meeting dialog box.

Enter the subject, location, time, date, and other information you need to schedule the meeting, and then notify the contact by sending an invitation (invitations are sent automatically during the process of creating the meeting). For more information about scheduling meetings, see Lesson 15, "Planning a Meeting."

ASSIGNING A TASK TO A CONTACT

As with mail messages and meetings, a contact must have an e-mail address to assign that individual a task. To assign a task to a contact, select the contact (tasks cannot be assigned to distribution lists), select **Actions**, and then select **New Task for Contact**. The Task dialog box appears. Enter the subject, due date, status, and other information, and then send the task to the contact, just click the Send Task button on the task's toolbar. For detailed information about assigning tasks, see Lesson 16, "Creating a Task List."

SENDING A LETTER TO A CONTACT

If you want to create a hard copy letter and send it using "snail mail" (meaning sending it using the postal system), Outlook can help you create the letter based on the information in a particular Contact's record. Outlook uses the Microsoft Word Letter Wizard to help you create a letter to send to a contact. Within the Word Letter Wizard, you follow directions as they appear onscreen to complete the text of the letter. (You must have Microsoft Word installed on your computer to use this feature.)

To send a letter to the contact, select the contact in the Contacts folder and choose **Actions,** and then select **New Letter to Contact.** Word opens the Letter Wizard onscreen. The Letter Wizard helps you format and complete the letter (see Figure 13.6). Just follow the onscreen directions to create the letter.

FIGURE 13.6
Use Word's Letter Wizard to create a letter to a contact.

CALLING A CONTACT

Another obvious way to communicate with a contact is over the telephone. For Outlook to dial the phone number for you, you must have a modem hooked to your computer that can dial out for you. With the right equipment, Outlook makes it easy for you to make a phone call to a contact by dialing the phone number for you.

For Outlook to manage your calls, you must have a modem hooked to your computer that can dial out for you. If you're in a networked environment that has access to a network modem pool, you can also dial out using your computer. The line you dial out on, however, must also be accessible by your telephone.

To initiate a phone call to a contact, select the contact in the Contact list and follow these steps:

1. Select **Actions**, point at **Call Contact**, and then select the appropriate phone number from the cascading menu that appears (all the phone numbers for the selected contact appear, including business, home, and fax). You can also click the **Dial** button on the Standard toolbar and select the appropriate phone number from the drop-down list. In both cases, the New Call dialog box appears (see Figure 13.7).

FIGURE 13.7
You can quickly initiate a telephone call to a contact using the Actions menu or the Dial button.

2. Click the **Start Call** button to allow Outlook to dial the contact's phone number using your modem.

3. The Call Status dialog box appears. Pick up your phone and click the **Talk** button in the Call Status dialog box. This engages the phone, and you can speak to your contact when they answer your call.

VIEWING A MAP OF A CONTACT'S ADDRESS

A useful feature Outlook offers is the capability to view an area map based on the address of a particular contact (requires an active Internet connection). This can be incredibly useful when you aren't sure where a particular contact is located.

To view a map of a contact's address, double-click the contact in the Contact list. The contact's record opens in the Contact dialog box.

 Click the **Display Map of Address** button on the Contacts toolbar. Microsoft Internet Explorer opens to the Microsoft Expedia Web site and displays a map based on the contact's address, as shown in Figure 13.8.

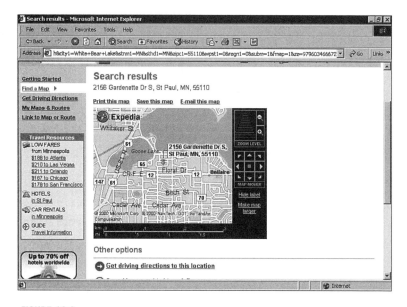

FIGURE 13.8
You can view a map of a contact's address.

You can zoom in and out on the map, and you can print a hard copy. When you are finished viewing the map and want to return to Outlook, simply close the Internet Explorer window.

In this lesson, you learned to create a Contacts list, view the list, and send mail to someone on your Contacts list. You also learned how to create a distribution list and view a map of a contact's address. In the next lesson, you will learn to navigate the Calendar, create an appointment, and plan events using the Outlook calendar.

LESSON 14
Using the Calendar

In this lesson, you learn how to navigate the Calendar, create appointments, and save appointments. You also learn how to insert an Office object, such as an Excel workbook, in an appointment.

NAVIGATING THE CALENDAR

You can use Outlook's Calendar to schedule appointments and create a task list. If necessary, Outlook can also remind you of appointments and daily or weekly tasks. You can schedule appointments months in advance, move appointments, cancel appointments, and so on. The Calendar makes it very easy to identify the days on which you have appointments.

To open the Outlook Calendar, click the **Calendar** icon in the Outlook bar, or select the **Calendar** folder from the Folder List. Figure 14.1 shows the Calendar in Outlook.

Outlook provides multiple ways for you to move around in the Calendar and view specific dates:

- Scroll through the Schedule pane to view the time of an appointment.

- In the Monthly Calendar pane, click the left and right arrows next to the names of the months to go backward and forward one month at a time. Click a date to display that day's information in the Schedule pane.

Monthly Calendar pane

Today's date

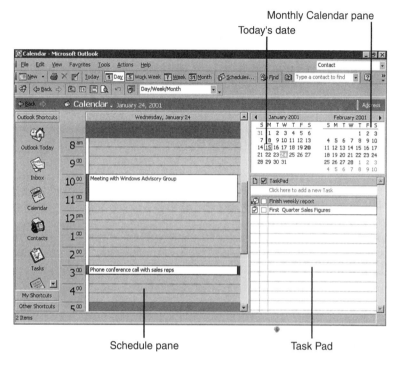

FIGURE 14.1

You can view all appointments and tasks at a glance.

Schedule pane   Task Pad

 TIP

> **Changing Calendar Views** You can change to different
> views of the Calendar by clicking the **Current View** drop-
> down arrow on the Advanced toolbar. Views including
> Active Appointments, Recurring Appointments, and By
> Category are available.

- In the monthly calendar pane, click a particular date on one of
  the months shown to display that date in the schedule pane.

- To view a different month in the Monthly Calendar pane,
  click the current month in the Monthly Calendar pane and
  select the name of the month from the shortcut list. Or you

can use the **Back** or **Forward** arrows to the left and right of the shown months (respectively) to go back or forward on the calendar.

- To view a week or multiple days in the Schedule pane, select them in the Monthly Calendar pane.

- To add a task to the Task Pad, click where you see **Click Here to Add a New Task** on the Task Pad.

- Use the scrollbars for the Task Pad to view additional tasks, if necessary.

TIP

Change the Date Quickly   To quickly go to today's date or to a specific date without searching through the Monthly Calendar pane, right-click in the Schedule pane and choose either **Today** or **Go to Date**.

CREATING AN APPOINTMENT

You can create an appointment on any day in the Outlook Calendar. When you create an appointment, you can add the subject, location, starting time, category, and even an alarm to remind you ahead of time.

Follow these steps to create an appointment:

1. In the Monthly Calendar pane, select the month and the date for which you want to create an appointment.

2. In the Schedule pane, double-click next to the time at which the appointment is scheduled to begin. The Untitled - Appointment dialog box appears, with the Appointment tab displayed (see Figure 14.2).

3. Enter the subject of the appointment in the **Subject** text box (you can use a person's name, a topic, or other information).

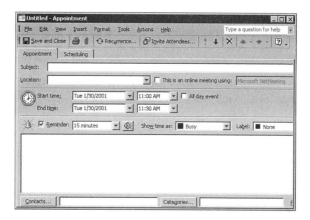

FIGURE 14.2
Enter all the details you need when scheduling an appointment.

4. In the **Location** text box, enter the meeting place or other text that will help you identify the meeting when you see it in your calendar.

5. Enter dates and times in the **Start Time** and **End Time** boxes (or click the drop-down arrows and select the dates and times).

TIP

> **Autodate It!**   You can use Outlook's Autodate feature: Enter a text phrase such as **next Friday** into the Start time or End time box, and then press **Enter**; Outlook figures out the date for you and places it into the appropriate box.

6. If you want your PC to let you know when you're due for the appointment, select the **Reminder** check box and enter the amount of time before the appointment occurs that you want to be notified. If you want to set an audio alarm, click the **Alarm Bell** button and browse your hard drive to select a specific sound file for Outlook to play as your reminder.

7. From the **Show Time As** drop-down list, you can select how the appointment time block should be marked on the calendar. The default is Busy. But you can also block out the specified time as Free, Tentative, or Out of Office. The drop-down list uses different colors and patterns to specify each of the different appointment types.

8. In the large text box near the bottom of the Appointment tab, enter any text that you want to include, such as text to identify the appointment, reminders for materials to take, and so on.

9. Click the **Categories** button and assign a category (or categories) to the appointment.

10. Click the **Save and Close** button to return to the Calendar.

The Scheduling tab enables you to schedule a meeting with co-workers and enter the meeting on your calendar. See Lesson 15, "Planning a Meeting," for more information.

Scheduling a Recurring Appointment

Suppose you have an appointment that comes around every week or month or that otherwise occurs on a regular basis. Instead of scheduling every individual occurrence of the appointment, you can schedule that appointment in your calendar as a recurring appointment.

To schedule a recurring appointment, follow these steps:

1. In the Calendar folder, choose the **Actions** menu, and then **New Recurring Appointment**. The Appointment dialog box appears, and then the Appointment Recurrence dialog box appears on top of the Appointment dialog box (as shown in Figure 14.3).

2. In the Appointment Time area, enter the **Start** and **End** times for the appointment. Outlook calculates the duration of the appointment for you.

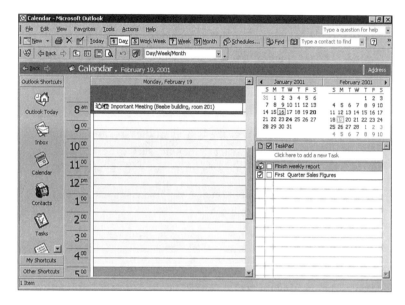

FIGURE 14.3
Schedule a recurring appointment once, and Outlook fills in the appointment for you throughout the Calendar.

3. In the Recurrence Pattern area, indicate the frequency of the appointment: **Daily**, **Weekly**, **Monthly**, or **Yearly**. After you select one of these options, the rest of the Recurrence Pattern area changes to provide you with appropriate options, such as days of the week for a weekly recurring appointment or day-of-the-month options for a monthly recurring appointment.

4. Enter the day and month, as well as any other options in the Re-currence Pattern area that are specific to your selection in step 3.

5. In the Range of Recurrence area, enter appropriate time lim-its according to the following guidelines:

   • **Start**—Choose the date on which the recurring appointments begin.

   • **No End Date**—Choose this option if the recurring appointments are not on a limited schedule.

- **End After**—Choose this option and enter the number of appointments if there is a specific limit to the recurring appointments.

- **End By**—Choose this option and enter an ending date to limit the number of recurring appointments.

6. Click **OK** to close the Appointment Recurrence dialog box. The Appointment dialog box appears.

7. Fill in the Appointment dialog box using the steps in the "Creating an Appointment" section already discussed in this lesson. When you finish providing all the details for the recurring appointment, click the **Save and Close** button to return to the Calendar.

The recurring appointment appears in your calendar on the specified date and time. A recurring appointment contains a circular double-arrow icon to indicate that it is recurring.

 TIP

Make Any Appointment Recurring   If you have already started creating an appointment and then would like to make it recurring, click the **Recurrence** button on the appointment's toolbar. The Appointment Recurrence dialog box opens.

PLANNING EVENTS

In the Outlook Calendar, an *event* is any activity that lasts at least 24 hours, such as a trade show or a conference. You can plan an event in the Calendar program to block off larger time slots than you would for normal appointments. In addition, you can schedule recurring events (such as a monthly seminar you attend that lasts all day).

To schedule an event, choose **Actions**, and then select **New All Day Event**. The Event dialog box appears (see Figure 14.4; it looks similar to the New Appointment dialog box).

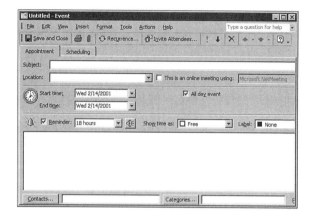

FIGURE 14.4
You can block out an entire day on the Calendar by scheduling an All Day Event.

Fill in the **Subject**, **Location**, **Start Time**, and **End Time** text boxes. Make sure the **All Day Event** check box is checked (that's the only difference between an event and an appointment). Click the **Save and Close** button to return to the Outlook Calendar. The appointment appears in gray at the beginning of the day for which you scheduled the event.

To schedule a recurring event, open a New All Day Event window and fill in the information as described earlier. To make the event recurring, click the **Recurrence** button in the Event window. The Event Recurrence dialog box opens; fill in the appropriate information and click **OK** (this dialog box is similar to the one for recurring appointments). Complete the information in the Event window, and then click the **Save and Close** button.

To edit an event or a recurring event, double-click the event in your calendar. Like a mail message or appointment, Outlook opens the event window so that you can change times, dates, or other details of the event.

INSERTING AN OBJECT

Outlook has the capability to insert an object, such as an Excel workbook or a file from any other Office application, into any Outlook item such as an appointment. For example, you might have an appointment to discuss some tax issues with your accountant and you have an Excel worksheet that details some of the information you want to go over. You can insert the Excel workbook right into the appointment. This makes it easy for you to view the data before you attend your appointment or even print the information.

You can insert an existing object into an appointment, or you can create an object within a message using the source application. For example, you could place an existing Excel workbook in an existing appointment.

To attach an existing object to an appointment in the Calendar, follow these steps:

1. Click the **Calendar** icon in the Outlook bar. Select **File**, **New**, **Appointment**. The new appointment will appear in the Outlook workspace. Position the insertion point in the appointment text box. This is where you will insert the Excel object.

2. In the appointment window, select **Insert**; then select **Object**. The Insert Object dialog box appears.

3. Choose the **Create from File** option (see Figure 14.5).

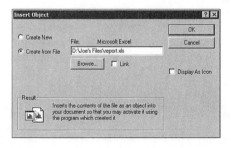

FIGURE 14.5
Insert an object, such as an Excel worksheet, into an Outlook task.

4. In the **File** text box, enter the path and the name of the file you want to insert. (You can use the **Browse** button and the resulting dialog box to search for the file, if necessary.)

5. Click **OK**. Outlook inserts the object into the Outlook item. The workbook or other inserted object actually resides inside a frame.

To edit an object, double-click within the frame, and the source application opens from within Outlook. Note that you'll still see your Outlook item and Outlook toolbars; however, you'll also see tools associated with the object's source application, which you can use to edit the object.

Figure 14.6 shows an Excel spreadsheet object within an Outlook appointment. Notice that the Excel toolbar and icons appear at the top of the Outlook window because an Excel object requires Excel's capabilities for editing.

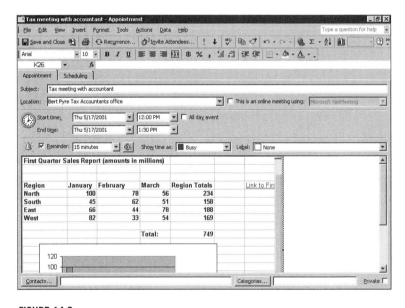

FIGURE 14.6
You can edit the object from within your Outlook appointment.

You can resize the object to suit your needs. First, select it, and a frame appears with eight small black boxes (called *handles*) on the corners and along the sides. To resize the object, position the mouse pointer over one of the black handles; the mouse pointer becomes a two-headed arrow. Click and drag the handle to resize the object.

When you change data in an embedded object, such as an Excel worksheet, remember to save the changes. Just click the **Save** button on the Excel toolbar (or the toolbar of the application that you are using to create the object). If you have resized an object in an item or inserted an object, remember to save the Outlook item (select **File**, **Save**).

Objects can also be inserted in tasks and meetings. Inserting objects enables you to have information related to a particular appointment, task, or meeting right at your fingertips.

In this lesson, you learned to navigate the Calendar, create appointments, and save appointments. You also worked with recurring appointments and the scheduling of events. In the next lesson, you will learn to create and schedule a meeting.

LESSON 15
Planning a Meeting

In this lesson, you learn how to schedule a meeting, enter attendees for a planned meeting, set the meeting date and time, and invite others to the meeting.

SCHEDULING A MEETING

Outlook enables you to plan the time and date of a meeting, identify the subject and location of the meeting, invite others to attend the meeting, and identify resources that will be needed for the meeting. You use the Calendar folder to plan and schedule meetings.

> **PLAIN ENGLISH**
>
> **Meeting**   In Outlook, a meeting is an appointment to which you invite people and plan for the inclusion of certain resources.

> **PLAIN ENGLISH**
>
> **Resources**   Any equipment you use in your meeting, such as a computer, a slide projector, or even the room itself.

To plan a meeting, follow these steps:

1. Click the icon for the Calendar folder on the Outlook bar. Then, in the Month pane, select the date on which you want to hold the meeting. To open a new meeting, select **Actions** and select **Plan a Meeting**. The Plan a Meeting dialog box appears (see Figure 15.1).

Attendees list   Green bar is starting time.

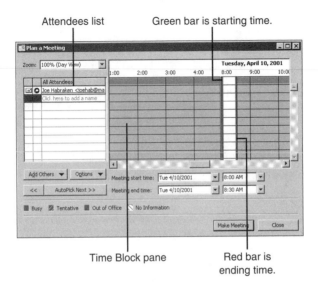

Time Block pane   Red bar is
                         ending time.

FIGURE 15.1
Choose the date and time of your meeting as well as the attendees.

2. To enter the names of the attendees, click in the **All Attendees** list where it reads Type Attendee Name Here. You can type a name into the box and then press **Enter**. Continue adding new names as necessary. Names that you type into the list do not have to coincide with records in your Contacts list, but if you include new names, Outlook will not have an e-mail address for those particular attendees when invitations are sent for the meeting.

3. A better way to invite attendees to your meeting is to click the **Add Others** button and choose the attendees from your Contacts list or other address book. This opens the Select Attendees and Resources dialog box, as shown in Figure 15.2. You can add attendees and any resources needed for the meeting in this dialog box. When you have finished adding attendees and resources, click **OK**.

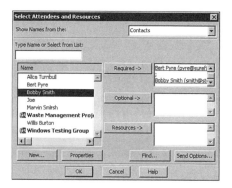

FIGURE 15.2
Attendees of the meeting and resources that will be needed can be added using the Attendees and Resources dialog box.

PLAIN ENGLISH

A Word About Adding Resources The Select Attendees and Resources dialog box enables you to add attendees and resources to a meeting. Because you probably don't list resources, such as overhead projectors, in your Contacts folder, you will have to type the resource names for the meeting as detailed in step 1 of this section (placing them in the Attendees list). In the case of resources, click the e-mail icon that appears to the left of the resource and select **Don't Send Meeting to This Attendee**. This keeps Outlook from trying to e-mail the resource. You can also use this option if you have listed attendees for the meeting who are not contained in your Contacts list.

4. To set a date for the meeting, open the **Meeting Start Time** drop-down list and select the date from the calendar, or just type the date into the text box. The ending date (in the **Meeting End Time** drop-down list) automatically shows the same date you set in the Meeting Start Time date box; you can change the End Time date if you want.

5. To set a start time for the meeting, do one of the following:

   • Open the **Meeting Start Time** drop-down list and select the time.

   • Type a time into the text box.

   • Drag the green bar in the Time Block pane to set the start time.

6. To set an end time for the meeting, do one of the following:

   • Open the **Meeting End Time** drop-down list and select the end time.

   • Type a time into the text box.

   • Drag the red bar in the Time Block pane of the dialog box to change the ending time of the meeting.

   After you select the date and time for the meeting, notice that the time grid to the right of each attendee's name shows the currently scheduled appointments that they have on the day of the meeting. The times blocked out in each attendee's grid are based on appointments and meetings in their Outlook Calendar. Outlook is able to check your corporate network and check attendee availability by using their calendars. If you have a conflict between your meeting time and an attendee's appointment, you can adjust the time of your meeting and avoid availability conflicts.

7. When you finish planning the meeting, click the **Make Meeting** button. The Meeting window appears, allowing you to refine the meeting details. Details on using this dialog box are described in the next section.

TIP

Check the Availability of Internet Colleagues   On a corporate network that uses Exchange Server, it's easy for Outlook to check other people's calendars to see whether they have a conflict with a meeting that you are planning. If you aren't using Outlook in an Exchange Server environment, you can also avoid scheduling conflicts by having people you invite use Internet e-mail to subscribe to Microsoft's Office Free/Busy Service. Outlook then periodically publishes a person's schedule to the service. All users that have subscribed can check the availability of participants using the service.

For more information about this service, go to http://www.microsoft.com/office/ on the Web.

TIP

Use AutoPick to Shift the Meeting Time Frame   You can click the **AutoPick Next** or **AutoPick Back** buttons to shift the meeting time (including the beginning and ending) to a half hour later or earlier, respectively. Each time you click one of the AutoPick buttons, the meeting shifts another half hour.

WORKING OUT MEETING DETAILS

After you plan a meeting, Outlook enables you to send invitations, identify the subject of the meeting, and specify the meeting's location. You enter these details in the Meeting dialog box.

When you schedule a meeting, as described in the previous section, you finish by clicking the **Make Meeting** button in the Plan a Meeting dialog box. When you do that, Outlook displays the Meeting dialog box with the Appointment tab in front (see Figure 15.3).

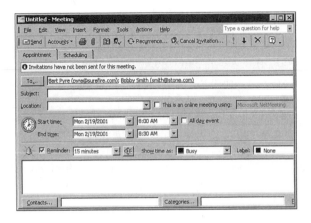

FIGURE 15.3
Specify the details related to the meeting in the Appointment tab of the Meeting dialog box.

Follow these steps to specify meeting details for a meeting you've already scheduled:

1. If you did not list the attendees in the Plan a Meeting dialog box, either click in the **To** text box and enter the names of the people that you want to attend the meeting, or click the **To** button to select the attendees from an address book or Contacts list.

2. In the **Subject** text box, enter a subject for the meeting.

3. In the **Location** text box, enter a location for the meeting.

4. (Optional) You can change the starting and ending dates and/or times in the Appointment tab. You also can choose the Attendee Availability tab to view the meeting in a format similar to that of the Plan a Meeting dialog box; make any changes to attendees, time, dates, and so on in the Attendee Availability tab.

5. (Optional) Select the **Reminder** check box and enter a time for Outlook to sound an alarm to remind you of the meeting. See Lesson 14, "Using the Calendar," for more information on using the Reminder feature.

6. (Optional) Enter any special text you want to send the attendees in the text box provided beneath the Reminder fields.

7. (Optional) If you plan to hold your meeting online using Microsoft NetMeeting, select the **This Is an Online Meeting Using** check box on the Appointment tab of the Meeting dialog box. Online meetings are scheduled the same as a face-to-face meeting; an online meeting, however, requires that you specify a Directory Server (this drop-down box is enabled when you select the online meeting check box) that will be used to connect the participants. In most cases, online meetings are held using Microsoft NetMeeting.

8. After you have entered all the required information for the new meeting, you can send invitations. However, before you send the invitations, you might want to make sure that the recipients reply to your meeting invitation. Select the **Action** menu and make sure that a selection check mark is next to **Request Responses**. If there isn't, click this selection to place a check mark next to it.

9. Now you can send the invitations; click the **Send** button. The meeting is saved and the Meeting window closes.

EDITING MEETING DETAILS AND ADDING ATTENDEES

You can edit the details of a meeting and change the date and time of the meeting at any time by opening the Meeting window. Opening the Meeting window also allows you to add attendees to the meeting.

Follow these steps:

1. In the Calendar folder, select the meeting date in the Monthly Calendar pane (any date that has scheduled appointments or meetings will be in bold on the Monthly Calendar pane). After you've opened the appropriate day, locate your appointment and double-click it to open it.

2. You can edit any information on the Appointment or Scheduling tabs.

TIP

> **Any Responses?**   Choose the **Tracking** tab of the Meeting window to see whether the people you invited to the meeting have responded to your invitation.

3. You can also add additional attendees to your meeting. On either the Appointment tab or the Scheduling tab of the Meeting dialog box, use the **To** or **Add Others** buttons, respectively, to open the Select Attendees and Resources dialog box.

4. Open the **Show Names from the** drop-down list and choose either **Contacts** or another address book (you can also add a new record to the selected address book by clicking the **New** button; see Lesson 12, "Using the Outlook Address Books," for more information).

5. Select any name in the list on the left side of the dialog box and click the **Required** or **Optional** button to specify attendance requirements.

6. Click the **New** button to add resources to the list; then remember to notify the person who is in charge of those resources of your meeting.

7. Click **OK** to close the dialog box and add the new attendees to your list.

When you have finished editing the meeting and/or adding new attendees, click the **Save and Close** button on the meeting's toolbar. A message box appears as shown in Figure 15.4, asking you whether you want to send the new meeting details to your original and added attendees.

FIGURE 15.4
Updating meeting details requires that you send new invitations to the meeting participants.

Because changing meeting details means that you also need to inform the attendees of any changes, click **Yes** to send the updated invitations. Attendees will be required to respond to the new invitation if the Request Responses option is selected on the Actions menu.

In this lesson, you learned to schedule a meeting, enter attendees for a planned meeting, set the meeting time, and invite others to the meeting. You also learned how to edit meeting details and invite new attendees. In the next lesson, you will learn to create a Task list.

LESSON 16
Creating a Task List

In this lesson, you learn how to enter a task and record statistics about the task. You also learn how to assign tasks to other users.

ENTERING A TASK

You can use the Tasks folder to create and manage tasks that you need to accomplish and don't want to forget about. You can list due dates, the status of a task, task priorities, and even set reminder alarms so your PC can keep you from forgetting a task entered in the list. To open the Tasks folder, click the Task shortcut in the Outlook Bar.

PLAIN ENGLISH

> **Task List**   A task list is a list of things you must do to complete your work, such as plan for a meeting, arrange an event, and so on. Various tasks might include making a phone call, writing a letter, printing a spreadsheet, or making airline reservations.

To enter a task, follow these steps:

 1. In the Tasks folder, click the **New Task** button on the toolbar or double-click any empty space on the Task list. The Untitled - Task dialog box appears (see Figure 16.1).

TIP

> **Use the Menu to Start a New Task**   To start a new task from the Task folder menu, select **Actions**, **New Task**.

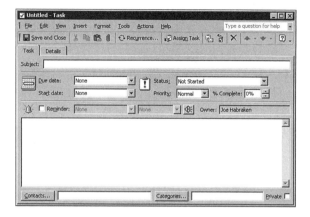

FIGURE 16.1
Enter data such as the subject of the task, due dates, and the task's priority.

2. On the Task tab, enter the subject of the task into the **Subject** box.

3. Enter a date on which the task should be complete, or click the down arrow to open the **Due Date** drop-down calendar, and then choose a due date.

4. Enter a start date, or click the down arrow to open the **Start Date** drop-down calendar, and then choose a start date.

5. From the Status drop-down list, choose the current status of the project: **Not Started, In Progress, Completed, Waiting on Someone Else,** or **Deferred**.

6. In the Priority drop-down list, choose **Normal, Low,** or **High** priority.

7. In the % Complete text box, type a percentage or use the spinner arrows to enter one.

8. (Optional) To set an alarm to remind you to start the task or complete the task, select the **Reminder** check box and enter a date and a time in the associated text boxes.

9. Enter any comments, descriptions, or other information related to the task in the comments text box located beneath the Reminder fields.

10. Click the **Categories** button and choose a category, if you want to assign the task to a particular category, or enter your own category in the text box.

TIP

> **Keeping a Task Private** If you are using Outlook on a corporate network that uses Exchange Server, your folders are kept on the Exchange Server and, to a certain extent, their contents can be viewed by other users. Select the **Private** check box if you don't want others to see information about a task that you are creating.

11. Click the **Save and Close** button when you're finished.

TIP

> **Create Tasks in the Calendar Folder** You can also create tasks on the Task Pad of the Calendar folder. Double-click the Task Pad to start a new task.

CREATING A RECURRING TASK

You can also create recurring tasks. For example, you might always have to hand in a weekly report every Friday; so why not schedule a recurring task that always reminds you to get that Friday report completed?

1. Double-click the Task Pad to open a new task window.

2. Enter the subject and other details of the task into the appropriate boxes.

| ↻ Recurrence... |

3. To make the task a recurring task, click the **Recurrence** button on the Task toolbar. The Task Recurrence dialog box opens.

4. You can set the recurrence of the task for Daily, Weekly, Monthly, or Yearly. After selecting an appropriate recurrence, such as Weekly, select how often the recurrence of the task occurs (see Figure 16.2).

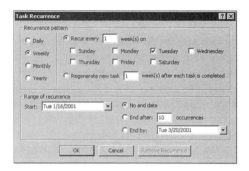

FIGURE 16.2
Set the recurrence pattern for a recurring appointment.

5. When you have finished setting the recurrence options, click **OK** to return to the task window.

6. Click **Save and Close** to save the new task. Recurring tasks are labeled in the task folder by a small circular arrow icon (letting you know that the task recurs).

Assigning Tasks to Others

You can also assign tasks to others, such as co-workers or subordinates. Assigned tasks appear in your Task folder; however, the person you assign the task to has control over the task or the changing of the task parameters. To assign a task, follow these steps:

1. Double-click the Task pane to open a new task window.

2. Enter the subject and other details of the task into the appropriate boxes.

3. Click the **Assign Task** button on the Task toolbar. A To line is added at the top of the task window (see Figure 16.3).

FIGURE 16.3
Use the To button to assign the task to people in your Contacts list.

4. Click the **To** button on the task and the Select Task Recipient dialog box opens.

5. Select the appropriate address book, such as your Contacts list, and then assign the task to a person or persons. Click **OK** to close the Recipient dialog box after you have finished assigning the task.

6. Click **Send** on the Task toolbar to send the task to the recipient or recipients. A message appears saying that, because you no longer own this task (because you have assigned it), no reminder will be assigned to the task (meaning you are not reminded if the task becomes past due). Click **OK** to close the message box.

Outlook sends the new task to the recipient or recipients. The task is actually sent as an e-mail message. When the recipient opens the e-mail message in their Outlook Inbox, two buttons appear at the top of the message, Accept and Decline (see Figure 16.4).

Accept task
    Decline task

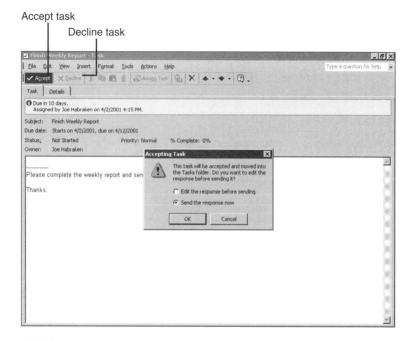

FIGURE 16.4
When a task recipient accepts the task it is moved to their Task list.

When the **Accept** button is selected, a message box appears (see Figure 16.4). This message box lets the recipient know that a response will be sent to the originator of the task and that the task will be moved to the Task Folder. To clear the message box, click **OK**. Now, when the recipient looks in the Outlook Task folder, they will find the task in the list.

If the task is declined (by clicking the Decline button), a message box appears saying that the task will be moved to the Deleted Items folder and that a message declining the task will be sent to the originator of the task (which in this case was you) and will appear in the originator's Inbox. Because a copy of the task is kept in your Task folder, you can open the task and assign it to another user.

VIEWING TASKS

As in any Outlook folder, you can change how you view tasks in the list using the Current View drop-down list in the Standard toolbar. By default, the Tasks folder displays tasks in a Simple List view. Following is a description of the views you can use to display the Tasks folder:

- **Simple List**—Lists the tasks, completed check box, subject, and due date.

- **Detailed List**—Displays the tasks, priority, subject, status, percent complete, and categories.

- **Active Tasks**—Displays the same information as the detailed list but doesn't show any completed tasks.

- **Next Seven Days**—Displays only those tasks you've scheduled for the next seven days, including completed tasks.

- **Overdue Tasks**—Shows a list of tasks that are past due.

- **By Category**—Displays tasks by category; click the button representing the category you want to view.

- **Assignment**—Lists tasks assigned to you by others.

- **By Person Responsible**—Lists tasks grouped by the person who assigned the tasks.

- **Completed Tasks**—Lists only those tasks completed, along with their due dates and completion dates.

- **Task Timeline**—Uses the Timeline view to display tasks by day, week, or month. Figure 16.5 shows the tasks assigned within one week.

CAUTION

Save What Settings?   Depending on the changes you make to a view, Outlook might display the Save View Settings dialog box asking whether you want to save the view settings before you switch to a different view. Generally, you'll want to discard the current view settings and leave everything the way you found it.

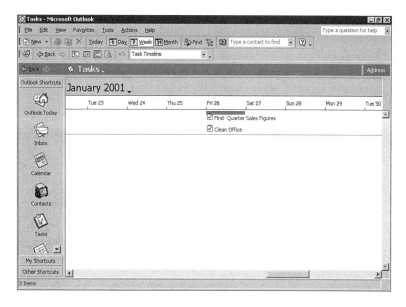

FIGURE 16.5
You can view your tasks in different views, such as the Task Timeline view.

MANAGING TASKS

When working with a task list, you can add and delete tasks, mark tasks as completed, and arrange the tasks within the list. You also can perform any of these procedures in most of the task views described in the previous sections. For information about printing a task list, see Lesson 19, "Printing in Outlook."

- To edit a task, double-click the task in the list. The Task dialog box appears.

- To mark a task as completed, click the check box in the second column from the left, or right-click the task and choose **Mark Complete** from the shortcut menu. Outlook places a line through the task.

- To delete a task, right-click the task and choose **Delete** from the shortcut menu.

- To assign an existing task to someone else, right-click the task and choose **Assign Task** from the shortcut menu. Fill in the name of the person to whom you want to assign the task (or use the To button to bring up the Select Task Recipient dialog box); after assigning the task, click the **Send** button to send the task to the recipient or recipients.

RECORDING STATISTICS ABOUT A TASK

You can record statistics about a task, such as time spent completing the task, billable time, as well as other information, for your own records or for reference when sharing tasks with your co-workers. This feature is particularly helpful when you assign tasks to others; you can keep track of assigned tasks and find out when they're completed.

To enter statistics about a task, open any task in the task list and click the **Details** tab. Figure 16.6 shows a completed Details tab for a sample task.

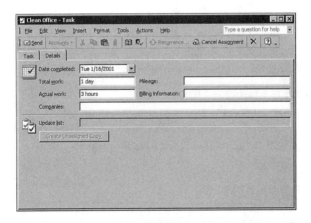

FIGURE 16.6
Fill in the statistics related to the completion of the task for later reference.

The following list describes the text boxes in the Details tab and the types of information you can enter:

- **Date Completed**—Enter the date the task was completed, or click the arrow to display the calendar and choose the date.

- **Total Work**—Enter the amount of time you expect the task to take.

- **Actual Work**—Enter the amount of time it actually took to complete the job. You can then compare the estimated time that you placed in the Total Work box with the actual time that it took (entered in the Actual Work box).

- **Mileage**—Enter the number of miles you traveled to complete the task.

- **Billing Information**—Enter any specific billing information, such as hours billed, resources used, charges for equipment, and so on.

- **Companies**—Enter the names of any companies associated with the contacts or with the project in general. Use semicolons to separate multiple names.

- **Update List**—Automatically lists the people whose task lists are updated when you make a change to your task. This is available only in situations where you are working in a Microsoft Exchange Server environment.

- **Create Unassigned Copy**—Copies the task so that it can be reassigned; use the button to send a task to someone other than an original recipient. This button is available only on tasks that you have assigned to other people.

Tracking Tasks

Outlook also enables you to track tasks that you assigned to others. You can even receive status reports related to a task that you have assigned to another person or persons. To track tasks, follow these steps:

1. On the **Tools** menu, click **Options**; the Options dialog box appears. Click the **Preferences** tab.

2. On the Preferences tab, click the **Task Options** button. The
Task Options dialog box opens (see Figure 16.7).

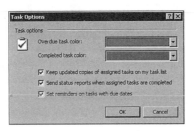

FIGURE 16.7
*Make sure that you set task options so that you receive updated tasks and status
reports for assigned tasks.*

3. To automatically track the progress of new tasks you assign
to others, make sure a check mark appears in the **Keep
Updated Copies of Assigned Tasks on My Task List** check
box.

4. To automatically receive notification when an assigned task is
complete, select the **Send Status Reports When Assigned
Tasks Are Completed** check box.

5. After you've made your selections, click **OK** to close the
Task Options dialog box, and then click **OK** to close the
Options dialog box.

TIP

> **Color Your Task List**   You can also set color options for
> overdue and completed tasks on the Task Options dialog
> box. Click the **Tools** menu, select **Options**, and from the
> Preferences tab, click the **Task Options** button.

In this lesson, you learned to enter a task and record statistics about
the task. You also learned to edit tasks and assign tasks to others. In
the next lesson, you will learn to use the Journal.

LESSON 17
Using the Journal

In this lesson, you learn how to create Journal entries manually and automatically and how to change views in the Journal.

CREATING A JOURNAL ENTRY

You can create a record of various actions so that you can track your work, communications, reports, and so on. In the Journal, you can manually record any activities, items, or tasks you want. For example, you might want to record the results of a telephone conversation.

You also can automatically record e-mail messages, meeting requests, meeting responses, task requests, and task responses. Additionally, you can automatically record activity related to documents created in the other Office applications: Access, Excel, PowerPoint, and Word.

The Journal is especially useful for recording information related to phone calls to and from people in your Contacts list. You can record information about the call, and you can also time the conversation and enter its duration (which is very useful information when you need to record billable-hours information for a particular client).

PLAIN ENGLISH

Journal A folder within Outlook that you can use to record interactions, phone calls, message responses, and other activities important to your work.

TURNING ON THE JOURNAL

As already mentioned, you can automatically or manually record items in your Journal. Before you can take advantage of the Journal, however, you must turn it on.

The first time you open the Journal folder (using the icon in the Folder List or the Journal icon in the My Shortcuts list on the Outlook bar), a message appears, asking whether you want to turn the Journal feature on. Click **Yes**. The Journal Options dialog box appears as shown in Figure 17.1.

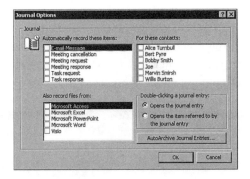

FIGURE 17.1
Click the check boxes in the Journal Options dialog box to have actions and events recorded automatically.

In this dialog box, you can specify what type of events you want to have automatically recorded in the Journal. Check boxes are provided to include e-mail messages, meeting requests, and other events that are received from people in your Contacts folder. To specify the items that you want automatically recorded, follow these steps:

1. In the **Automatically Record These Items** list, check those items you want Outlook to automatically record in your Journal. (The items recorded correspond with the people selected in the list of contacts in step 2.)

2. In the **For These Contacts** list, check any contacts you want automatically recorded in the Journal. Outlook records any items selected in step 1 that apply to the selected contacts.

3. In the **Also Record Files From** list, check the applications for which you want to record Journal entries. Outlook records the date and time you create or modify files in the selected programs.

4. When you have completed your selections, click the **OK** button. The Journal opens. It is now ready to automatically record the items that you chose in the Journal Options dialog box.

Suppose that you wanted Excel sessions to be automatically recorded in the Task list. You would make sure that Excel was selected in step 3. Then, whenever you work in Excel, that event is recorded. Figure 17.2 shows a Journal entry for an Excel event.

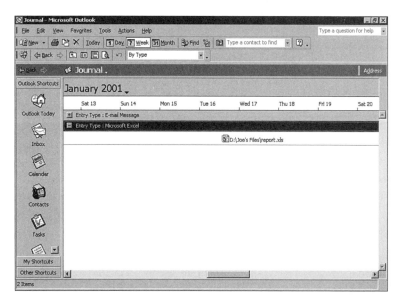

FIGURE 17.2
Journal entries for applications, such as Excel, are recorded automatically when you work in that application.

RECORDING AN ENTRY MANUALLY

You can also record items in the Journal manually using existing items such as e-mail messages. For example, you might add an e-mail message to the Journal that is not normally recorded (because you didn't select messages from that particular contact as something you want automatically recorded in the Journal).

To create a Journal entry manually, follow these steps:

1. In the Inbox folder (or any other folder in Outlook), select the item you want to record in the Journal and drag it onto the Journal folder icon in the Folder List (or drag it onto the Journal icon on the Outlook bar). The Journal Entry dialog box appears (see Figure 17.3).

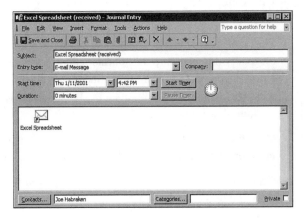

FIGURE 17.3
Drag an item onto the Journal icon, and the Journal Entry dialog box opens.

2. The information in the Subject, Entry Type, Contact, and Company boxes and some other information is entered for you from the selected task, contact, or other selected item. However, you can change any of the statistics you want by entering new information into the following text boxes:

- **Subject**—Displays the title or name of the Journal item.

- **Entry Type**—Describes the item based on its point of origin, such as a Word document, a meeting or appointment, and so on.

- **Company**—Lists the company or companies associated with the contacts.

- **Start Time**—Displays the date and time of the meeting, appointment, or other item.

- **Start Timer**—Like a stopwatch, the timer records the time that passes until you click the Pause Timer button.

- **Pause Timer**—Stops the timer.

- **Duration**—Enter the amount of time for completing the item.

- **Shortcut box**—Displays a shortcut to the item you originally dragged onto the Journal icon to create a new entry (such as a Calendar appointment, a contact, or a message). You can actually open the item by double-clicking the shortcut icon.

- **Contacts**—Lists the name(s) of any attendees, contacts, or other people involved with the selected item.

- **Categories**—Enter or select a category that you want to assign to the Journal entry.

3. Click **Save and Close** to complete the Journal entry.

If you want to create a new Journal entry, but you don't have a contact, a task, an e-mail, or other item that you want to use to create the entry, you can create a Journal entry from scratch (meaning it is not associated with any existing Outlook item such as an e-mail message). For example, you might want to create a Journal entry that holds information related to a phone call that you have made. Follow these steps:

1. Change to the Journal folder.

2. Choose **Actions**, and then select **New Journal Entry** or double-click any empty portion of the Journal pane. The Journal Entry dialog box appears.

3. Enter the subject for your new journal entry.

4. Select the type of entry you want to make; in this case, the default is already set to Phone Call. Leave the Journal Entry window open on your desktop.

5. Make your phone call; you can actually have Outlook dial the phone call for you using the **AutoDialer** icon, which can be accessed on the toolbar in the Contacts folder (click the **AutoDialer** icon, and then select **New Call**; use the **Contacts** drop-down list in the New Call dialog box to specify the contact that you want to call, and then click **Start Call**).

6. When your call is answered, click the **Start Timer** button in the Journal Entry window. Type any notes that you want to record during the phone conversation in the entry's text box.

7. When you finish the call, click the **Pause Timer** button. Notice that the duration of the call is entered in the Duration box. To save the Journal entry, click the **Save and Close** button.

CHANGING JOURNAL SETTINGS

You might find that when you started the Journal for the first time, you didn't configure that many events to be automatically recorded by the Journal. No problem; you can return to the Journal settings and change the options related to the automatic recording items in the Journal.

In the Journal folder, choose **Tools**, **Options**. The Options dialog box appears. Click the **Preferences** tab if necessary, and then click the **Journal Options** button. The Journal Options dialog box appears.

You can also choose to have your Journal entries AutoArchived. Click the **AutoArchive Journal Entries** button, and then choose a folder on your computer where you want to have the Journal Archive file stored (selecting the default folder is your best bet). Then, click **OK** to complete the process (for more information about the AutoArchive feature, see Lesson 21, "Archiving Items").

When you have finished making changes to the Journal options, click **OK** to close the Journal Options dialog box. Then, click **OK** to close the Options dialog box.

VIEWING JOURNAL ENTRIES

By default, the Journal folder displays information in the Timeline view and By Type, as shown in Figure 17.4. However, you can display the entries in various views, as described in the following list. To select a particular view, click the **Current View** drop-down button on the Advanced toolbar.

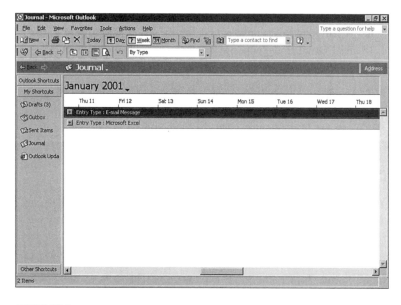

FIGURE 17.4
The default Journal view is the Timeline view.

KEEPING TRACK

> **Save Settings?**   As in other views, Outlook might display the Save View Settings dialog box to ask whether you want to save the view settings before you switch to a different view. You're probably getting used to this dialog box by now.

- **By Type**—In Timeline view, this option groups Journal entries by type, such as e-mail messages, meetings, Word documents, and so on. Double-click a type to display its contents, and then position the mouse pointer over an entry to view its contents or name. When you switch to the Journal in the Type view, a Journal Options dialog box appears. This dialog box allows you to specify which e-mail messages will be recorded in the Journal, based on the contact they are received from. This dialog box also allows you to select which application use will also be recorded in the Journal, such as Excel, Word, or Access.

- **By Contact**—In Timeline view, this displays the name of each contact that you selected in the Options dialog box. Double-click any contact's name to view recorded entries.

- **By Category**—If you've assigned categories to your Journal entries and other items, you can display your Journal entries by category in the Timeline view.

- **Entry List**—Displays entries in a table with columns labeled Entry Type, Subject, Start, Duration, Contact, and Categories.

- **Last Seven Days**—Displays entries in an entry list but includes only those entries dated within the last seven days.

- **Phone Calls**—Lists all entries that are phone calls.

In this lesson, you learned to create Journal entries manually and automatically and to change views in the Journal. In the next lesson, you will learn to create notes.

LESSON 18

Using Outlook Notes

In this lesson, you learn how to create, sort, and view notes.

CREATING NOTES

If you've ever used a Post-it note to remind yourself of tasks, ideas, or other brief annotations, Outlook's Notes are for you. Notes are similar to paper sticky notes. You can use Notes to write down reminders, names, phone numbers, directions, or anything else you need to remember. In Outlook, all notes are kept in the Notes folder. You'll have to remember to look at the folder so you can view your notes.

 TIP

> **The Long and Short of It**   You can enter pages and pages of text if you want. As you type, the page scrolls for you; use the arrow keys and the Page Up and Page Down keys to move through the note's text. Keep in mind, however, that the purpose of the note is a quick reminder, or information that you will eventually transfer to one of the other Outlook items, such as an appointment or task.

To create a note, click the **Notes** folder on the Outlook bar and then follow these steps:

1. In the Notes folder, choose **Actions**, and then select **New Note** or double-click an empty spot in the Notes pane. A new note appears, ready for you to type your text.

2. Enter the text for your note (see Figure 18.1).

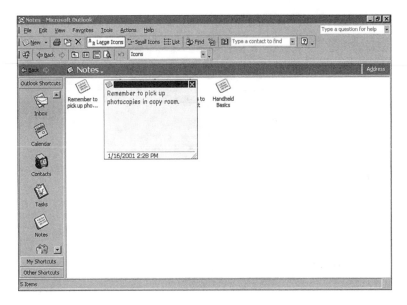

FIGURE 18.1
A note automatically includes the date and time it was created.

3. When you finish, click the **Close (x)** button to close the note. You can reopen a note and edit the text as you need to.

If you press Enter after entering text in the note, you create a line break and you create a title, of sorts, at the same time. Only the text before the hard return displays when the note is closed. If you do not add a hard return but enter the note text so that it automatically wraps from line to line, the entire note text appears below the note in Icons view.

SETTING NOTE OPTIONS

You can change the default color and size of your notes. You also can change the default font used for your notes. To set note options, follow these steps:

1. In the Notes folder (or in any of the Outlook folders), choose **Tools, Options**. The Options dialog box appears. On the

Preferences tab, click **Notes Options**; the Notes Options dialog box appears (see Figure 18.2).

FIGURE 18.2
You can customize your notes.

2. The Notes Options dialog box enables you to change the color, size, and font for your notes. Using the Color drop-down box, you can change the color to yellow, blue, green, pink, or white. The default is yellow.

3. Open the **Size** drop-down list and choose **Small**, **Medium**, or **Large** for the size of the notes. The default is Medium.

4. To change the font, click the **Font** button. The Font dialog box appears. Change the font, font style, size, color, and other options, and then click **OK**.

Managing Individual Notes

To open an existing note, double-click it in the Notes folder. You can edit the text in an open note the same as you would edit any text. To move a note, drag its title bar. You can delete, forward, or print notes; you can change the color of individual notes; and you can specify categories for your notes. You can also drag the notes to the Windows desktop and arrange them there.

Click an open note's Control Menu button (click the very upper left of the note) to display a menu with the following commands:

• **New Note**—Creates a new note but leaves the first note open.

• **Save As**—Enables you to save the note and its contents.

- **Delete**—Deletes a note and its contents. (You also can delete a note by selecting it in the Notes list and pressing the **Delete** key.)

- **Forward**—Enables you to send the note as an attachment in an e-mail message.

- **Cut, Copy, Paste**—Enables you to select text from the note and cut or copy it to the Clipboard. The Paste command enables you to paste items on the Clipboard at the insertion point in the note.

- **Color**—Choose another color for the individual note.

- **Categories**—Enter or choose a category.

- **Print**—Print the contents of the note.

- **Close**—Closes the note. (You can also click the **Close** (**x**) button in the note's title bar.)

VIEWING NOTES

The Notes folder provides various views for organizing and viewing your notes. The default view is Icons, but you can change the view using the Current View drop-down list on the Advanced toolbar. Figure 18.3 shows the Notes folder in the default view.

You can choose to display your Notes folder in any of the following views:

- **Icons**—Displays the notes as note icons with the message (or a portion of the message) displayed below the icon.

- **Notes List**—Displays the notes in a list, showing the title and note contents in the Subject column, the creation date and time, and the categories.

- **Last Seven Days**—Displays all notes written in the last seven days, by subject, creation date, and categories.

- **By Category**—Displays the categories; double-click a category to show its contents.

- **By Color**—Displays notes by their color. Double-click a color to display the notes.

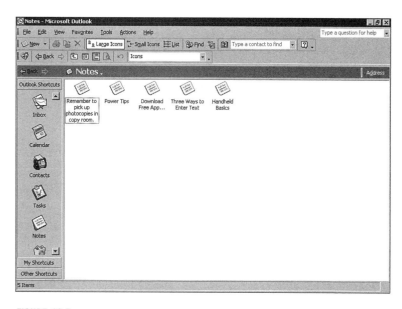

FIGURE 18.3
This view displays the notes in Icons view.

In this lesson, you learned to create and view notes. In the next lesson, you will learn to print in Outlook.

LESSON 19
Printing in Outlook

In this lesson, you learn how to print items in Outlook, change the page setup, preview an item before printing it, and change printer properties.

CHOOSING PAGE SETUP

In Outlook, before you print, you choose the print style you want to use. Each folder—the Inbox, Calendar, Contacts, and so on—offers different print styles, and each style displays the data on the page in a different way.

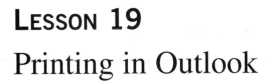

PLAIN ENGLISH

Page In Outlook, this is the area of the paper that will actually be printed on. You might, for example, print two or four pages on a single sheet of paper.

PLAIN ENGLISH

Print Style The combination of paper and page settings that control printed output.

You can choose from Outlook's built-in print styles, modify the default print styles, or create your own print styles. These lists show the default print styles available for each folder. To access the print styles for a particular item, select **File**, **Print**. The Inbox, Contacts, and Tasks use the Table style and the Memo style; the Journal and Notes use only the Memo style.

- **Table Style**—Displays data in columns and rows on an 8 1/2×11 sheet, portrait orientation, 1/2-inch margins.

- **Memo Style**—Displays data with a header of information about the message and then straight text on an 8 1/2×11 sheet, portrait orientation, 1/2-inch margins.

The Calendar folder provides the Memo style as well as the following styles:

- **Daily Style**—Displays one day's appointments on one page on an 8 1/2×11 sheet, portrait orientation, 1/2-inch margins.

- **Weekly Style**—Displays one week's appointments per page on an 8 1/2×11 sheet, portrait orientation, 1/2-inch margins.

- **Monthly Style**—Displays one month's appointments per page on an 8 1/2×11 sheet, landscape orientation, 1/2-inch margins.

- **Tri-fold Style**—Displays the daily calendar, task list, and weekly calendar on an 8 1/2×11 sheet, landscape orientation, 1/2-inch margins.

- **Calendar Details Style**—Shows the currently displayed Calendar items and the body text of each item (such as an appointment) in a list format.

The Contacts folder provides the Memo style as well as the following styles:

- **Card Style**—Two columns and headings on an 8 1/2×11 sheet, portrait orientation, 1/2-inch margins.

- **Small Booklet Style**—One-column pages that print the contacts in a format similar to mailing labels by placing multiple contacts on a page. This style can be printed in Portrait or Landscape mode.

- **Medium Booklet Style**—One column that equals 1/4 of a sheet of paper. Four pages are on one 8 1/2×11 sheet of paper, portrait orientation, with 1/2-inch margins.

- **Phone Directory Style**—One column, 8 1/2×11 sheet of
  paper, portrait orientation with 1/2-inch margins.

> **CAUTION**
>
> **Will Page Setup Change My View?**   No matter how you
> set up your pages, it will not affect your view of tasks,
> calendars, or other Outlook items onscreen. Page setup
> applies only to a print job.

You can view, modify, and create new page setups in Outlook. To view
or edit a page setup, follow these steps:

1. Change to the folder for which you're setting the page.

2. Choose **File** and then point at **Page Setup**. A secondary menu
   appears that lists the available print types.

3. Select the print type you want to view or edit, and the Page
   Setup dialog box appears (see Figure 19.1).

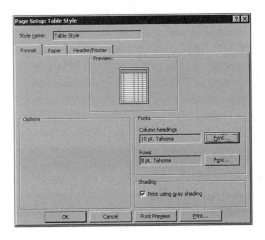

FIGURE 19.1
Customize the print style to suit yourself.

4. Click the **Format** tab to view and/or edit the page type, to
   choose options (in some cases), and to change fonts.

5. Click the **Paper** tab to view and/or edit paper size, page size, margins, and orientation.

6. Click the **Header/Footer** tab to view and/or edit headers for your pages.

PREVIEWING BEFORE PRINTING

To make sure an item looks the way you want it to look, you can choose to preview it before printing it. If you do not like the way an item looks in preview, you can change the page setup.

Open the folder that contains the item that you want to print preview. You can then open the item in the Print Preview view in any of the following ways:

- Click the **Print Preview** button in the Page Setup dialog box.

- Choose **File** and then select **Print Preview**.

- Click the **Print Preview** button on the Advanced toolbar.

- Click the **Preview** button in the Print dialog box.

Figure 19.2 shows a calendar and task list in Print Preview. You can change the page setup by clicking the **Page Setup** button; the Page Setup dialog box appears. Click the **Print** button to send the job to the printer. Click the **Close** button to exit Print Preview and return to the Outlook folder.

TIP

Enlarge the View   When the mouse pointer looks like a magnifying glass with a plus sign in it, you can click to enlarge the page. When the mouse pointer looks like a magnifying glass with a minus sign in it, you can click to reduce the view again.

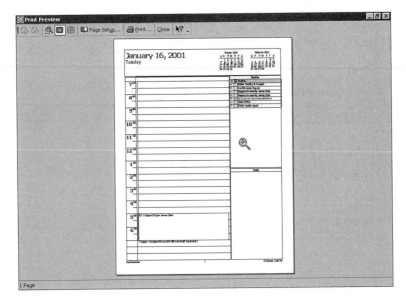

FIGURE 19.2
Preview the item before printing it.

PRINTING ITEMS

After you choose the print style and preview an item to make sure it's what you want, you can print the item. You can indicate the number of copies you want to print, select a printer, change the print style or page setup, and set a print range.

When you're ready to print an item, follow these steps:

1. Choose **File**, and then select **Print** or click the **Print** button on the Standard toolbar. The Print dialog box appears, as shown in Figure 19.3.

2. Your default printer appears in the Printer area of the dialog box. If you have a different printer connected to your system that you would like to use, choose a different printer from the **Name** drop-down list.

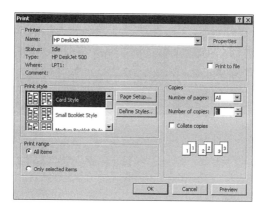

FIGURE 19.3
Set the printing options before printing the item.

3. In the Print Style area, choose a print style from the list. You also can edit the page setup (with the **Page Setup** button) or edit or create a new style (with the **Define Styles** button).

4. In the Copies area of the dialog box, choose **All**, **Even**, or **Odd** in **Number of Pages**, and enter the number of copies you want to print. This function is useful if you are going to print on both sides of the paper (this is called manual duplexing). You print the even pages, and then flip the sheets over in your printer and print the odd pages. Click the **Collate Copies** check box if you want Outlook to automatically assemble multiple copies.

5. Set the print range with the options in that area. (The Print Range options vary depending on the type of item you're printing.)

6. Click **OK** to print the item.

PRINTING LABELS AND ENVELOPES

A handy Outlook feature is the capability to print mailing labels and envelopes from your Contacts list. To take advantage of this feature, you also need to have Microsoft Word installed on your computer. Creating form letters, mailing labels or envelopes is called a *mail merge*. Basically, in Word, you create some type of main document (such as mailing labels, envelopes, and so on) that holds field codes that relate to the information you keep on each contact, such as name or address.

To actually start the merge process, open your Contacts folder and select **Tools**, **Mail Merge**. The Mail Merge Contacts dialog box opens (see Figure 19.4) and allows you to specify both the contacts for the merge and the Word document into which the contact information is merged. Using the option buttons at the top of the dialog box, you can specify that all the contacts or selected contacts are included in the mail merge. If you want to have only certain fields included in the mail merge, you can create a custom view of your Contacts folder (discussed in Outlook Lesson 4, "Using Outlook's Tools") before starting the Mail Merge.

After you specify the various options in the Mail Merge Contacts dialog box (see tip that follows) and click **OK**, you are taken to Word, where the mail merge is completed. To use this feature, you will need to have Microsoft Word installed on your computer. Just follow the steps provided by the Word Mail Merge Wizard to complete the merge process.

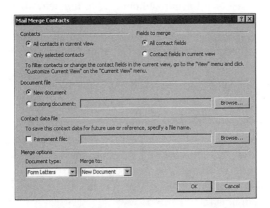

FIGURE 19.4
Contact data can be merged with a document in Word for mass mailings.

TIP

> **Setting Up a Mail Merge from Outlook**   The Mail Merge
> Contacts dialog box (refer to Figure 19.4) provides sev-
> eral options for customizing your mail merge using your
> Outlook Contacts. If you select the **Permanent File** check
> box, you can specify a filename and have your Contacts
> list saved as a data document for use in future Word
> mail merges (you won't have to start the merge from
> Outlook in the future if you select this option). You can
> also specify the type of document that Word creates dur-
> ing the mail merge using the Document type drop-down
> list. You can create form letters, mailing envelopes, and
> mailing labels.

SETTING PRINTER PROPERTIES

Whether you're printing to a printer connected directly to your computer or to a printer on the network, you can set printer properties. The
properties you set apply to all print jobs you send to the printer until
you change the properties again.

PLAIN ENGLISH

> **Printer Properties**   Configurations specific to a printer
> connected to your computer or to the network. Printer
> properties include paper orientation, paper source,
> graphics settings, fonts, and print quality.

CAUTION

> **Access Denied?**   If you cannot change the printer prop-
> erties to a network printer, it's probably because the net-
> work administrator has set the printer's configuration
> and you're not allowed access to the settings. If you
> need to change printer properties and cannot access the
> printer's Properties dialog box, talk to your network
> administrator.

To set printer properties, open the Print dialog box (by choosing **File**, **Print**). In the Printer area, select a printer from the Name drop-down list, and then click the **Properties** button. The printers' Properties dialog boxes differ depending on the make and model.

Most likely, you'll be able to set paper size, page orientation, and paper source using options on a Paper tab in the dialog box. In addition, you might see a Graphics tab, in which you can set the resolution, intensity, and graphics mode of your printer. A Fonts tab enables you to set options on TrueType fonts, font cartridges, and so on. You might also find a Device Options tab, in which you can set print quality and other options. For more information about your printer, read the documentation that came with it.

In this lesson, you learned to print items in Outlook, change the page setup, preview an item before printing it, and change printer properties.

INDEX